Lisa,

Thank you for all
your help — you
are a real —

In Christ,
Walter Kallad(?)

Ro. 8:32

the big why

BY

WALTER HALLAM

Harrison House
Tulsa, OK

13 12 11 10   10 9 8 7 6 5 4 3 2 1

The Big Why
ISBN 13: 978-1-60683-014-7
ISBN 10: 1-60683-014-7

Copyright © 2010 by Walter Hallam
601 Delany Road
La Marque, TX 77568

Published by Harrison House, Inc.
P.O. Box 35035
Tulsa, Oklahoma 74153
harrisonhouse.com

CONTENTS

FOREWORD

Why? Why did the Lord allow my wife to die young with cancer? Why didn't the Lord protect my son when he went off to war? Why did the accident take the life of my child? Why is the one word that everyone will ask at some point in their lives - and the answer often determines how they will respond to God's purpose in their lives, or how they will respond to others.

People are often taught to never question God. However, no teacher ever suggests that their students not ask questions. For when there are no questions asked, there will be no answers given. After all, the Bible is an answer book to the world's problems and for your personal needs. It is normal to ask why. It is even better to understand why.

At some point in life you will have at least one major incident or personal event that will cause you to question why it happened. As you begin to ponder this bad experience, you will either turn to God for the answers, or as some have, you will turn from Him in anger or frustration. It is time that someone with an experience gives us the answer to the "Big Why".

What you are about to read will absolutely change your life! One of the most complicated questions to answer is why bad things happen to good people. The question becomes further complicated when wondering why the Lord would allow a child or a young teenager to die because of an accident or terminal illness. Pastor Walter Hallam, the author of this book, has lived through a nightmare that no parent wants to experience – the loss of his teenage daughter in a plane accident. I first heard Walter share this incident, through tears, several years ago. But it was a supernatural visitation from Christ Himself that answered Walter's difficult questions.

When Walter shared this incredible, life changing visitation with me and revealed the deep revelation that Christ gave him, it was literally the greatest revelation I had ever heard, answering numerous complicated questions concerning death and the reasons why bad things happen to good people.

This is one of those books that, once you begin to read it, you will have difficulty putting it down. The insights it contains will help bring peace and freedom to many of you who have experienced various forms of sorrow, especially due to the loss of a loved one.

I have known Pastor Hallam for many years and have been blessed to minister at his wonderful, growing church in La Marque, Texas. He has spoken in our main yearly conference and is a "revelator of God's Word". Every message he preaches leaves a spiritual imprint on the hearts and minds of the listeners. The insights in this book will do the same for you.

Perry Stone, Jr.

PART ONE

THE
JOURNEY
THERE

Chapter 1

THE GLORY OF KINGS

God gave me an inquisitive nature. Since I was young, I've wanted answers to the big questions about life. *The Big Why* is in response to my early-on quest to understand tragedies in life—why they happen and even how to prevent them. I happen to believe that desiring and searching for truth is not something peculiar, however, to only me or a handful of others.

The Bible says that **"the glory of kings is to search out a matter"** (Proverbs 25:2 NKJV). It is the destiny of God's created beings—who have been what the Bible refers to as "born again"—to be **"kings"** to God, their Father. (Revelation 1:5,6.) It is part of our spiritual DNA, especially as Christians, to be searchers of truth.

Having been created in the image of God, we *all*—Christian and non-Christian, alike—have it built into our spiritual design to pursue truth. Whether or not we yield to that yearning and look for our answers in the right place is a matter of choice.

POINTED IN THE RIGHT DIRECTION

We look for our answers in the right place when we look to the God of the Bible as the source for our understanding to questions that have no "natural" answer. When we look to the Creator, the one who made us with a plan in mind, we are on course for truth. (Jeremiah 29:11.) When we take knowledge from the wisdom of God's Word, that wisdom truly becomes power and a deep spiritual understanding in our lives.

At a very early age, I was pointed in the right direction and to the right source—God and His Word—in attempting to satisfy my inquisitive mind and searching soul. I grew up in an atmosphere of dynamic, vibrant Pentecostal faith. I grew up around those who believed in God's Word *and* His ability to give spiritual understanding to the mysteries of life. I witnessed His power manifested through "gifts of the Spirit," which are part of God's spiritual ability for the Church today. I grew up in a strain of Christians who were *very* gifted.

As a boy, for instance, I attended the meetings of William Branham, who prophesied with precision accuracy. He supernaturally discerned the diseases of complete strangers, administered divine healing to crowds of thousands, and raised the dead. He was known for supernatural manifestations like the light that hovered over him during a water baptism or the halo which was photographed above his head. The glory of God appeared in some of his meetings in the form of a pillar of light by his side. I was there when some of this happened in Branham's meetings in Louisiana. As a boy—a young boy in Shreveport, Louisiana—*I was there.*

Like I said, I've always been a person with a lot of questions. I do believe that the deep subject matter of my questions and the intensity of my pursuit were uncommon for my age. The answers I sought were for the *big* why's of life—things that were way beyond my years. I think part of that was because of my call to the ministry. And also, it had to do with certain experiences that caused me to view life differently. I mean, if you ever die—literally die—and are brought back to life, things are never quite the same.

A PIVOTAL EXPERIENCE

I drowned at a Christian youth camp when I was eight years old. I was actually dragged from the bottom of the lake and resuscitated. I often wondered why I was spared when other people weren't. Other people had drowned but they didn't get to come back, even when their circumstances had been much less dangerous and threatening than mine. But I was recovered from the lake's bottom—*I lived!*

For the kids who couldn't swim, there was a little roped off place in the water that was not much more than a wading area of a couple feet deep. For the kids who could swim, there was an area with a pier where the water was maybe ten feet deep. Kids were allowed to jump from the pier into the lake. Well, the pride of this eight-year-old wouldn't stand for being stuck in the wading area while all those other boys could go in the deep end. I thought, *If they can do it, I can.* I ran over to the pier and leaped into the lake, realizing as soon as I did, that you have to know how to swim to get back out of the water.

I started attempting to swim while still in the air, before I ever hit water. When I did make contact, I sunk like a rock right to the lake's bottom. I came back up thrashing at the water, arms flailing wildly, only long enough to spit up water and get a gulp of air; and then back under I went. Three times I managed to make it back to the lake's surface before it all became too much.

The lifeguard—figuring that nobody would have been dumb enough to do what I had just done—thought I was playing around and cutting up like the rest of the boys. So right under the lifeguard's nose, I drowned.

THE BIG WHY

Before losing consciousness, my mind, the best way I can describe, went into warp speed. Even at eight years of age, everything I had ever done in life appeared to flash right by me—*zip, zing.* It's hard to explain. I laughingly tell people now that when you're only eight years old, it goes by so fast that you need to have reruns. But then, when I got close to the door of eternity, there was a slowing down.

I remember thinking sometime during those fleeting seconds, *God, if You'll help me, if You'll save me, I'll live for You.* I was repenting. I was doing everything that a little kid could do; and I didn't even know what I was repenting of. And then I drowned.

Apparently a girl had seen me out in the water struggling, and noticed that I hadn't come back up. She started screaming and yelling, and then the lifeguard came after me. The next thing I knew, I was lying on the pier, spitting up water and mud. And so I came to wonder, *Did God spare me for a reason?*

Today, of course, I'm a minister. From about twenty countries, there have been hundreds of thousands of people with whom I've had the privilege of praying the prayer of salvation. Whoever that lifeguard volunteer was will have a share in that reward of souls when we get to heaven one day.

Why did I drown in the first place? Why did I survive when others did not survive? I've shared that I became a minister. Was that why? My daughter Angela, who did not survive a plane crash, was already a minister—a junior youth pastor—at seventeen years of age. How many souls could she have reached had she recovered? Thousands? Millions? Why did she not live through it? These are good questions that this book will help to answer.

GODLY UPBRINGING

I came into this world with a particular divine purpose, or calling, on my life. I believe God has designed every person for meaning, purpose, and fulfillment—that there is a plan for each of us. The "call" of God on my life gives context to the answers that I offer in this book.

> *For I know the thoughts and plans that I have for you, says the*
> *Lord, thoughts and plans for welfare and peace and not for evil,*
> *to give you hope in your final outcome.*
>
> *Jeremiah 29:11* AMP

While the plan for a person's life is fixed and implanted deep within, it is in the mind of God, man's Creator, first; that's where it begins. This call may be a call to business, to married life, or it could be a specific call to ministry, like mine was.

I believe that if someone has a call of God on his life, he is born into the world with it, just as Jeremiah came into the world with a particular call on his life. That's what God told him: "Before I formed thee in the belly I knew thee; and before thou camest forth out of the womb I sanctified thee, and I ordained thee..." (Jeremiah 1:5). This kind of selective service or assignment doesn't come from a grandparent, a parent, an uncle, or a close friend. It has to come from God. We don't usually function in a call placed on our lives right away. There is a time of preparation, of fine-tuning, of maturing, of developing the kind of character needed for the task. While people in our lives can't *call* us into the work of the Lord, they can have something to do with preparing us for the divine appointment on our lives.

THE BIG WHY

I had an advantage in this area, as well. I grew up in a pastor's home. My mother and father pastored a Spirit-filled, Pentecostal church in Jasper, Texas, for nearly fifty years. My father did a live radio broadcast fom a local radio station around seven or eight o'clock on Sunday mornings before he went to the church to preach. My mother and I would go with him. She would play the piano and I would sing. I have six brothers and sisters who love the Lord, but none of them did this. I don't know why I was drawn into the ministry, but I'm the only one of my siblings in full-time ministry today. I was six years old when I was on the radio, and the broadcast was for an hour. Daddy must have done that for fifteen to twenty years every Sunday morning, and so he was well-known in the area.

From an early age, I can remember always wanting to serve the Lord, wanting to live for Him. But I had my own plans—I wanted to be a millionaire and a deacon, in that order. As soon as I was old enough and in a position to do so, I began working toward my goal of being a millionaire. I worked until my brains felt like they were oozing out of my ears. I kept busy making money, but at the same time I tithed, gave offerings, lived a moral life, and served God to the best of my understanding. I mean, I always knew from the time I was a little boy that I was going to be rich—I knew it. Though I was poor growing up, I never doubted for a minute—one day I'd be rich. The *last* thing I wanted to be was a preacher. Yet, somehow—even though I didn't want to be—I knew I was going to be a minister. How it was going to happen, I didn't know; but I knew it was going to happen. Little did I know that one day God would interrupt my life and say, *Quit your job and everything you're doing. Get ready because I'm going to launch you into the world for My service.*

When I was about twelve years old, a very old man in a small, country, Pentecostal church called me out of a crowd and began to speak to me (through a "prophetic gift"), saying, "I see you playing musical instruments—musical instruments. You're going to be playing musical instruments." He poured some oil in my hands and he prayed over me. I've said I grew up around "very gifted" Christians. One afternoon, after playing seventh-grade football, I came into the house and sat down at the piano. I can't explain it other than to say that a light simply clicked on the inside of me, and I started playing the piano. I've been playing for over forty years now. I can play half a dozen musical instruments and never had the first lesson. I can just play them, and it literally happened just like that. The light came on. Music theory came alive on the inside of me. I played and sang, and even traveled for years as part of a little singing group. I believe that is part of God's "divine call" on my life.

All through high school, I lived for God. I was very active in athletics, winning many high school athletic awards in baseball and football in the state of Texas. When I was seventeen, I went to college to play baseball. After a year, I became disillusioned with the college scene; and it wasn't because I was ill-prepared in my upbringing. I had grown up in a good, strong, controlled, Christian environment. I have no nightmares to share about my upbringing. My childhood was great and so were my parents. But one day after my first year in college, I went home and told my parents that I had joined the Air Force—which sounded like a crazy decision.

A CRAZY DECISION, IN THE PUBLIC EYE, AND RED HAIR

My mother and my father, a former Marine, were extremely upset because I hadn't told them what I planned on doing. There was no justifiable reason for it. I was simply disillusioned with college. I enlisted in the Air Force and I went through technical school, focusing on avionic navigation in electronics.

An aptitude test was part of the requirements, and I apparently tested high in the area of administration. As a result, I was offered a position as a law clerk working in the Judge Advocate's Department. Out of about ten thousand men, only twelve of us were given this opportunity.

After training for JAG, I wound up at England Air Force base in Alexandria, Louisiana, where I could drive back and forth to my home in about two and a half hours. I easily traveled back and forth to East Texas every week, even a couple of times a week. While the decision to go into the Air Force had appeared to be a big mistake, as it turned out God was preparing me for something. Many *why's* in life are answered after we've gone through certain times and experiences if we will allow God to do His work. God sees the *big* picture of our lives while we normally only see the "snap shot" of the moment.

In the long run, my college classes at four or five different schools and in the Air Force were mostly in business or real estate, which I really liked. I finished my degree at Oral Roberts University where I got my Masters in Divinity.

I continued to live for the Lord, even while I was in the military. That's not saying that I was perfect, but I sure was trying. When I came out of the Air Force, I went to work for my father for just a short time. He, even while pastoring for many years, owned a large laundry and dry cleaning business with a lot of employees and some major commercial customers such as hotels and hospitals.

I was familiar with being in the public eye, as I worked in my dad's very successful business, sang and played music, ministered in the church, taught Sunday school and youth classes, and remained very active in athletics. I also came from a family that had an eye-catching uniqueness of a different sort. I have bright red hair. My mother and daddy both had red hair; all four of my grandparents had red hair; and I had six brothers and sisters with red hair. So we were an entirely red-headed family. There were seven brothers and sisters plus their parents with red hair and blue eyes…and we were always dressed nicely. When we walked into a restaurant, we stood out from the crowd. We got a lot of attention whether we liked it or not.

I believe the reason that red-headed kids are accused of having hot tempers, and often do, is because they get picked on or singled out from the time they're little. They often don't know which one is happening—if they're being picked on or if they're just being singled out. A red-headed child is often looked at as unique. Statistically, there are fewer than one red haired person for every 100 people.[1] There can be fifty kids in a classroom and if one of them has red hair, I'll guarantee that kid's hair is going to get mentioned. The teacher is going to comment or someone else will say something and it doesn't have to be something negative. It just happens. But when you're a child, and especially if you're a boy, anything that singles you out causes you to become defensive. You learn to fight at a young age. For me, that explains the mystery of why red-headed people are branded as having hot tempers.

THE BIG WHY

My red hair helped me to become acclimated to public scrutiny and eyeballing. It helped prepare me for a life of being in the public eye. It had its part to play in the hot temper I once had and the kind of strong-willed fighter I am now. Being a fighter is a good thing when fighting for the right cause and against the real enemy. So often there is something about ourselves that causes us to ask God, *Why? Why did You give me this? Why did You make me this way?* What so many people dislike about themselves or even about life in general can turn out to be a blessing.

When I came out of the military, my brother Gary and I had the only argument that we ever had as far as I can recall. My dad broke us up and said, "Walter, go to the house and cool off." On the way home, I turned on the car radio and was still fuming mad, having been a hot-tempered fighter at that time. There was an advertisement on the radio for a purchasing agent needed at Louisiana Pacific. In my state of anger, I went home, changed clothes, and drove straight to that plant to apply for the job.

When I walked into the office, there were applicants sitting everywhere. It was a great job being offered—head buyer for LP in their southern division at a large mill. I had zero experience for such an opportunity. Regardless, the office manager came through and saw me, came over, and inquired, "Hey, aren't you one of those red-headed Hallam boys?" It happened just like that.

I replied, "Yeah, I'm Walter Hallam."

He said, "Walter Hallam, come here." I went into his office.

He asked, "What are you doing here?"

"Well, I'm here applying for that job I heard advertised on the radio about a purchasing agent."

He responded, "Really? What are you doing?"

I quickly told him I had gotten out of the military and had been in the Judge Advocate's Office. I had been trained as a court reporter to run a ten-key calculator and I could type very fast. He went to get the plant manager, brought him in, and hired me on the spot. I had no experience. He hired me right on the spot for a great job with great benefits—the whole thing. I could hardly believe it. I was twenty-two years old.

It happened just like that. I went to work for LP in management without a degree and without any similar work experience. After a couple of years, I went to work for one of LP's vendors. They ultimately offered me fifteen percent of the business' profit and asked me to be a salesman for them. I was making about $400,000 a year back in the late seventies. That company gave me a nice business incentive to keep me there. I never had any trouble making money. I worked at this new position for a while. Eventually I sold my part of the company and started a battery business.

A BUSINESSMAN AND A PASTOR

During this time, I became engaged to a beautiful young lady whom I had known since we were teenagers in my hometown. Although I am three years older than her, our families had known each other for many years. We grew fond of each other and then fell madly in love. Somehow I'd always known I was going to get her to marry me—I didn't want anyone else!

The Big Why

Soon I married my wife Cindy, and together we started a church in the little town of Pineland, Texas, population of about six hundred. Our work there began with just one couple in a trailer home. I thought it was only going to be a youth outreach. As it turned out, we bought and renovated an old auto parts store into a church. My wife and I started pastoring this church, and we grew to almost one hundred people. That was just about the biggest church in that town. I was only twenty-seven at the time.

I thought that this was what I was going to do forever. *Well, this is me. I'm going to be a businessman and work and pastor this church.* This was all I had ever really known about church because my parents had done the same thing—owned their own business and pastored. Their church never had over 150 people in it at one time, yet it was quite powerful and effective. To have over one hundred people back then was a big deal.

Cindy and I pastored the church in Pineland for about two and a half years. I ministered Sunday mornings and Wednesday nights there and some Sunday nights for my dad. I was still assisting my dad in his church, and I would speak at youth functions. During that time I started a second company—another battery company. I did this to supplement the mill supply, the first company, but it grew to be more. I started selling batteries by the semi-tractor trailer load, and even developed my own brand of battery. I eventually sold my part in the industrial supply business, but my own little company kept growing and growing. I continued pastoring in Pineland.

One day, after praying for about an hour, the Lord spoke to me very powerfully and said, *This church is like a nursery for what I have for you to do. I'm training you for what I've called you to do.* I had a pastor friend who I believed I was supposed to turn the church over to and install as the new pastor there, as God had something else for me to do.

LOOKING FOR A CITY

I spent the entire month of July of 1984 traveling and ministering with my family—in Texas, Colorado, Idaho, Utah, and even Wyoming. Our business had provided us with enough income to take some time off. I had a lot of connections through my father. I thought, *Well, maybe I'm supposed to be a traveling preacher—an evangelist.* But I was very unsettled in my heart during this month. I loved the preaching part; but as for the *traveling*, I knew that wasn't what God was calling me to do.

For four weeks we traveled and preached and prayed about God's will for our lives. My experience had been that when you wait on the Lord, you generally need to be real busy while waiting. I believe that when you don't know the will of God, your job is finding the will of God instead of just sitting back waiting for something to fall out of the sky.

After that month of praying and preaching in several churches, my family and I returned to East Texas. Cindy and I went to Houston to hear an elderly minister in his nineties at a meeting of about forty or fifty ministers at a big hotel. At the end of the meeting, the minister said to us, "If you'd like for me to pray for you, come up and get in this line." I really felt like I was there for a reason, so Cindy and I went and stood in the line. When the man came to us, he put his arms around us and said, "I feel like the Lord is going to give you a 'word of direction' within the next twenty-four hours." That got my attention. I thought, *Well, praise the Lord. Man, I think that's really God!*

So I stayed awake for the next twenty-four hours, trying every way I could to receive this word, because I didn't know what God wanted me to do. Cindy and I were looking—that Abraham effect, you know, where Abraham "*looked* for a city which hath foundations, whose builder and maker is God" (Hebrews 11:10, emphasis mine). It was interesting that financially and in other ways, everything was going right for us. As far as physical needs being met, we were not desperate; we just wanted to know the will of God. But in twenty-four hours, I hadn't received any special direction from the Holy Spirit for our lives. So I thought, *Well, maybe I just missed it.*

About two weeks later I got a telephone call from a man who had been standing in line behind Cindy and me in Houston. He said, "My wife and I were standing behind you when you were prayed for, and old Papa Mayes said that you were going to have a word from God in twenty-four hours. Did you get your word?"

I said, "No, I didn't get it. I guess I missed it."

This fellow was really quiet on the phone, and then he said, "Well, that's because I think, Walter, I think God gave me the word to give to you; and I just didn't do it."

My response was, "Spill the beans, guy. What is it?"

He said, "We pastor a little church down here in Texas City that has just a handful of people. My wife and I want to go into missions work; we want to move back to Europe. We feel like God told us right out of the blue to tell you to come take this church."

When that man presented this to me, it changed my life. It is still really precious to me to this day. I calmly responded by saying, "Well, praise the Lord. Let me talk to my wife about it," but bells were going off on the inside of me. My heart was just about to leap out of my chest. This church had about fifty people in it who met in a little, old gym, and Cindy and I had left the church in Pineland with around one hundred in attendance. But I was excited. This was in November 1984.

I telephoned my wife after this conversation. She was really quiet, and then asked, "Walter, what do you think?"

I said, "I don't know what to think, Cindy." I was in the office, and my battery company was doing really well. I told my wife, "I don't even know what to say. We'll just pray about it now." And so we did.

My parents were still in our hometown of Jasper, and my dad wanted me to take his church one day. Cindy's mother and grandmother were there; her father had died when she was two. I had been the captain of the football team, and she had been the head twirler in the high school we attended. We had known each other basically our entire lives, and that hometown was what we knew. This other place—Texas City—was about three hours away; but because it was on the coast, it felt like a *world* away. I didn't like seagulls. I didn't like oysters. I didn't like saltwater. I didn't like the beach. I had never vacationed on the beach. I would sunburn badly. It just didn't work for me to move to Texas City.

Cindy and I prayed about it. Truthfully, the minute this pastor told me he believed we were supposed to take his church, I knew that we would. Five minutes before that conversation, that would have been the most foreign thing on the planet for me to do. I knew instantly, however, that this was going to happen—we were going to do it.

Regretfully, I Believe It's God

Cindy agreed to it. I couldn't and wouldn't have done it if my wife hadn't agreed with me. I'll never forget when I later asked her, "Well, what do you think? Honey, tell me what you think."

Cindy answered, "Well, regretfully, I believe it's God." I'll never forget that. It was the funniest thing to me. I didn't hesitate one second. The minute she said it, I wasn't going to let her change her mind. I went after it. I still didn't sell my company for eighteen months—*because I wanted to have something to come back to in the event I had missed God*. It wasn't God that I didn't trust.

So we moved and started pastoring that church on January 3, 1985. It was an eclectic congregation of a handful of people meeting in the gym of an old, decrepit, closed-down elementary school in Texas City, Texas. Texas City and La Marque, Texas, where we are now, is basically one town, one area for sure.

We took over a church that had disintegrated, going down to almost nothing. For my first time of ministry in Texas City, I chose a Wednesday night in December, believing that a church can be judged more by its night services than its day services. Sunday morning has the largest crowd, but the strength of a church shows up in the evening services. Sticking to this conclusion, I found the strength of this church to be twelve to thirteen souls. I was blown away. I realized that Cindy and I were about to move to *next-to-nothing*, but we did anyway.

At the end of seven weeks of preaching every message at that church, about two hundred people were in attendance. The man who had invited me to come pastor decided that he didn't want to leave. So he came up with a plan where he would be the pastor and I would be the preacher. He said, "I want you to preach, but I'm going to pastor the church." Well, that was against what I understood to be the Biblical order for a church government and certainly not the reason I had moved to Texas City.

It was an unscriptural situation and nowhere close to what I was called to do. Cindy and I never would have moved there under those conditions or under that premise. I expressed that to this other minister, telling him, "I've got to reconsider my whole position."

That day my mother called, and I told her what was going on. She, a great Spirit-filled woman who is now in heaven, told me about a revival at her church. A young and upcoming evangelist, a young man under Kenneth Hagin's training, was ministering. She said, "Walter, I just feel like God would have you come and hear this guy. You should come and hear him. I believe God has a special word for you."

I said, "Well, Mama, I can't just drop everything and go up there, you know."

She said, "I just believe the Lord is telling you to come here. You really need a word from God." Of course, I knew that Mama really wanted me to move back home.

I said to her, "Well, I'm going to do it then. I'm going to come." I have always believed that we should be led by the Spirit of God, and I'll do whatever I can to give Him the opportunity to speak to me.

So Cindy and I took our children and headed to the meeting in our Suburban. It was normally about a three hour drive but because it was so rainy and the wind was blowing so hard it made our trip at least an hour longer than normal. We had to look to the Lord for mercy that Thursday evening! It rained and hailed so badly that I had to pull off the road a couple of times. I thought, *Man I need to turn around and go home. I can't believe I have my kids out in this stuff.* But I kept going anyway.

The church service was already in full progress when we finally arrived. We got there late, went in, and sat on the back row. I'll never forget the message the young minister preached from the book of Daniel, but there was no particular word in it for me—nothing directional. I thought, *Well, I'm going to at least say hello to this guy, since I drove over three hours to hear him.*

After the church service was dismissed, I got up and began to walk to the front of the auditorium to introduce myself and tell him I had enjoyed his message. I got about ten feet from where he was in front of the pulpit and he looked at me and said, "You, yeah, you right there. I have a word for you from God." He literally grabbed me, laid his hands on me, and started ministering in prayer and prophecy. He was a very aggressive sort of minister, and full of God.

I began to shake as he spoke powerful words of direction to me, although to my knowledge he had never heard of me before. He said, "There's a city, city. What's this city thing? City."

I had just moved seven weeks before to Texas City.

He continued, "There's a city, city, city, city. There's something about the city." Then he stated, "There's a region. There's an area. God's called you over an area as a spiritual leader."

Then he said something so powerful to me that I'll never forget as long as I live. This stranger, who didn't know me from Adam, said, "Now if men call you and they accept you, bless them. If they reject you, you dust your feet as a witness." He continued, "Now, if God calls you to an area, it's a different kind of call. You can't leave unless God tells you to leave. You can't go unless God releases you from that area."

There is a great spiritual difference for ministers when they are called by men to a church versus being called by God. It has to do with plans and purpose from God. God can use any minister who teaches, preaches, and loves the people—they obey the Lord. But sometimes, God will "call" a specific person to an area or city for a powerful work of God that affects the region. I believed then and now that was what God was asking me to do.

This young minister was warlike, wild, and powerful; and he wouldn't stop. He was just what I needed in order to hear from God. I am so hard-headed sometimes. By the time that evangelist was through with me, I knew exactly what God was telling me. Sometimes God's voice is inside of His voice when He's talking to us. God can say one thing and we can hear twenty things at one time. God talks in paragraphs; He doesn't just talk in a word. One of His words carries the content of an entire paragraph to me.

I drove back to the coast, and on Monday morning I sat down and talked to the pastor of the church in Texas City, telling him, "I've received a word from God, a word of direction." I told him exactly what it was. I told him I was going to speak in the same area because that's the reason I was there. I told him I wouldn't hurt him in any way as long as he pastored his church. If anyone from his congregation came to hear me and decided to leave his church, I would require that this individual go back and meet with that pastor personally. I would require that he notify his pastor that he was leaving, and to give him the honor that was due. This pastor's people couldn't just come to my church and join the church; I wouldn't let that happen. As a result, he was actually happy for me to go because his church had grown to the biggest it had ever been during the seven weeks I had been speaking there.

THAT CHURCH IN THAT FUNERAL HOME

On the first Wednesday night of March, 1985, I held a service in my house. With ten other adults, my wife and I started our new church. God had given me direction. Out of John 10:10, we called the church Abundant Life. Jesus said, "I am come that they might have *life*, and that they might have it more *abundantly*." Today, we have grown to four thousand active members.

The following Sunday, I rented a room at the Quality Inn on the Texas City dike, the largest man-made dike in the world. I held church there for seven weeks, and then the hotel wanted us out. We had reached about thirty people in attendance by then. I couldn't find any place in the area to have a church, because I knew we had a *big* church *in* us. I knew from the first day when there were twelve people that we were a *large* church.

I went all over the area looking for a place to meet but I couldn't find one until I came across a funeral home that was used only when necessary. It was in La Marque, a predominantly African-American town separated by railroad tracks from Texas City. Here I was from Jasper, Texas, looking at a funeral home for holding church services in a small coastal town. Ringing in my ears was the taunting thought: *The absurdity of God to call me to La Marque, Texas!*

But God led me to the funeral home. The owner offered to let us use the chapel rent-free on Sundays and purchase it if we liked it.

The chapel seated 120 people. The owner of the funeral home told me many years later, while standing in one of the five foyers of our present church, "My wife and I have laughed for years about the time I told you the chapel held 120 people. You were real nice, but said, 'You know, I don't think that's going to be large enough for us.'" He added, "And you had just told me that you only had twenty-five or thirty members in your church. I went home and told that to my wife and we just laughed about it. You were such a dreamer, you know. We've laughed about that conversation for years." Never give up on your dreams!

We moved into the funeral home, but the owner wouldn't let us put a sign outside because he was afraid it would hurt his business. He was afraid that people would think it was a church instead of a funeral home. I said, "I've been in a lot of churches that feel like funeral homes, but I haven't been in a lot of funeral homes that feel like churches." We packed that place out. People literally stood around the walls.

The news got out about the church that met in the funeral home. This wasn't too long after the Jim Jones cult murders and the Jonestown mass suicides of the late seventies. I remember how I was affected by all of that, because my family was considered well-accepted, even high profile, where we grew up. I never wanted to be considered a cult or fanatical person. I've always tried to be "normal" and "spiritual" at the same time.

Here I was trying to start a church, and I'll never forget what happened one day. My wife and I and our oldest daughter, Catherine, who was about three, walked into a restaurant. I was carrying Angela, who is in heaven today. She was just an infant then. When we entered the restaurant, a lady reached over and pulled her children close. I heard her say to someone, as if she were afraid of us because she thought we were in a cult, "That's those people who have that church in that funeral home." That was the day I almost left the ministry, battling temptation. I thought, *I'm not going to do this to my family—to my kids. I'm not going to put them through this.* I came so close to going back to East Texas that day because of that lady's reaction and the feeling I had of being looked at like a cult leader of some kind. I was so mad and hurt that I just didn't know what to do. God does not lead your life by public opinion polls. Every man has a "call" of some kind on them. Your mission in life is to discover your divine purpose, then do it!

People made a lot of jokes about us for a while, but it didn't take me long to get over that. I decided, "This is the will of God, so I don't care what they say. I'm here for the duration." The devil harassed my wife and me over this. He said, *Your daughters are going to grow up and be by themselves. They're going to be lonely. They're going to be little misfits. They will never have any friends. You had better pack up and go back to where you came from.* These were very tormenting thoughts. You can never go forward and backward at the same time. Commit, submit, and permit God to help you go beyond your fears and distractions. Almost every success in life has a moment of defeat before it becomes a victory.

I took a stand and came up with a plan for overcoming my fears for our children. Every Sunday morning, I'd have the parents bring their children into the sanctuary. I would announce, "We're going to receive a penny offering. Can we have the children come bring an offering today?" I'd ask the church to say with me, "*One day* it will take five minutes to do this!" The church would literally scream out the "five minutes" part of the confession, *"Five minutes!"* I'd say, "One day it will take five minutes just to receive a children's offering because there'll be so many children in this church." All the kids would come up front, bringing their coins, and we'd time it. We did this for years, and I'll never forget the first Sunday that it took five minutes to do it.

We have hundreds of children in our church today. My daughters did not grow up lonely and they did not grow up misfits. Today our daughters have college degrees from the University of Houston and Regents University in Education, Divinity, English, and Business. Oh, the goodness of God!

We stayed in the funeral home for nine months, until we outgrew it. We had to find a new place and the La Marque area did not have a lot of choices. There was a big food chain that had an old warehouse behind one of its stores, so I leased about five thousand square feet of warehouse. Every Sunday morning I could smell the baking going on inside the tiny store bakery. Let me preach against demons, but don't make me compete with donuts! You just can't win against that.

YOU RECKON IT'S ANY GOOD?

We were in the warehouse for almost nine months. On Easter Sunday morning, 1986, this certain fellow came to church. That evening the church treasurer, who was from Arkansas originally, called. He had a slow Arkansas drawl. I can still hear his words in my ears when he said, "Pastor, are you sitting down?"

I said, "Yeah."

He said, "You know so-and-so who came to church today?"

I asked, "That older gentleman?"

He said, "Yeah, he put a check in the offering today for $20,000! You reckon it's any good?"

I said, "Well, I don't know if it's any good or not (he didn't look like the kind of fellow who had that kind of money), but let's run it through the bank to find out." It was the largest single offering I had ever received up until then in the ministry.

Sure enough, it was good. So I called this fellow, and he said, "Well, I retired from one of the chemical plants out here and I just believe in what you're doing. God just told me to give $20,000 this morning, so I wrote a check for $20,000."

I asked the Lord, "What in the world will I do with this?" It was the most money I had ever received in a church offering. I had made a lot of money in business, but in church I'd never had anybody give $20,000. So I thought, *Good night! What do I do now?* And the Lord said to me really powerfully, *That's the seed for your first church building in La Marque.* Everything in life begins with a seed!

This Is the Ugliest Land!

Now before this offering was ever given, I had started looking for land. I got up every morning around 7:00 A.M., five days a week, for a solid year. I drove every road and every street in Galveston County and prayed over it. I figured there was a place for us, and I believe in places. The Bible says that "the whole creation groans and labors with birth pangs together until now," and that "the earnest expectation of the creation eagerly waits for the revealing of the sons of God" (Romans 8:19,22 NKJV). I believe that there are places on Earth where God Himself chooses to build churches, where nature travails and groans, wanting that kind of purpose. I do not believe that every place where people assemble is necessarily a place chosen by God. God was emphatic in the Bible about where He put the ark, where the Temple was built, where certain altars were built, where certain wells were dug, and so on. While I believe that the Lord will meet us anytime, anyplace, I see the building of a house of God as a divine thing. It's a predestined sort of thing—a plan that God has.

So I would drive and pray for hours every day, five days a week. One day, I drove through La Marque to a place called Hitchcock— another scantily-populated, at that time predominantly African-American town. I drove down this little country road to a piece of undeveloped terrain boasting nothing but patches of salt grass, a run-down shack, a weathered barn, and some rusted barbwire fence. It all looked so old and forlorn; and I thought, *This is the ugliest land!* The Lord said to me plainly, *Buy that piece of land right there!*

I stopped my car and looked at that area and said out loud, "God, this is the ugliest property I've ever seen in my life, and I'm on a dirt road." The Lord said to me again, *Buy that piece of property!*

I didn't even know for sure where I was, but I managed to make it back to the interstate; I hadn't traveled too far. I found a realtor in town and asked him to come out and look at the property with me. He asked, "What do you want this property out here for, Preacher?"

I said, "Well, I'm going to build a great church out here."

He commented, "I wouldn't recommend it, you know, on a dirt road."

I responded, "You know, I wouldn't recommend it either; I'll be honest with you. But I have to tell you that this is what I'm supposed to do."

I bought those two acres—paid cash for them. They were my first two acres, and they cost about $18,000. Afterwards, the offering of

$20,000 on Easter Sunday came in. I said to the church, "You know, the church has a piece of property we've bought out here, and I think we ought to build a building. Somebody has already given $20,000. That's our seed money. I'm going to start receiving money for the building now."

As our church was now a year old, we had probably 100 to 120 faithful church attendees. In Galveston County, Texas City and La Marque, there were hardly any churches that I knew of with over four hundred people attending on Sunday. None. Not Baptist. Not Methodist. There weren't any in the immediate area around us that had even hundreds of people on Sunday. People didn't come to where we were in Galveston County to go to church. They came there to party and to work in the factories. There are a lot of professional people in that area now. Closer to Houston, we run into the Johnson Space Center—NASA—on the southeast side of Houston, but our particular area is definitely a blue collar area.

After that gentleman gave the $20,000, we started a building program, and people started giving. In about six months we had $100,000 or so, a ton of money, phenomenal for that little group of about one hundred.

We broke ground and built a fourteen thousand square foot facility. It was 100 feet by 100 feet with about 4,000 square feet upstairs. The building would seat about four hundred people. We dedicated the new church building on Easter Sunday of 1987. We paid cash for it except for about $145,000 or so, and we paid that off within about a year. A little over two hundred people attended and we had a lot of visitors. I even poured a concrete parking lot. We were about the only church in the county with a concrete parking lot at that time.

THE HOLY SPIRIT SAYS TO BUY IT ALL

I held my first big conference in 1987. I invited Dr. Lester Sumrall, who did not know me at all. He was just returning from Israel, and had received the vision just that week for the Feed the Hungry End-Time Joseph Program. When we finally drove up to the parking lot of the church, Dr. Sumrall got out of my car and looked around.

He asked, "Do you own that land over there?"

I said, "No, sir, we just own these two acres."

He asked, "How about that land over there?"

I said, "No, sir."

He stated, "Well, you need to buy it all. The Lord says for you to buy it all. You're going to need it." He continued, "There's something different about you. You need this land. You need all of it." What a powerful word!

THOSE THAT GO AND DO IT

That day Dr. Sumrall and I talked. "Dr. Sumrall, the reason I asked you to come is because I need to know about world missions. I don't know anything about it. I grew up in a little, East Texas town, and I don't know anything about world missions. The only thing I know about missions is jail ministry. I used to preach in the jail. I feel like during my prayer time the Lord told me that you're the leading world evangelist today, so that's why I called you."

He just sat there for a minute and stared at me. I thought I was going to die. We were in a world-famous seafood place in downtown

Galveston. Dr. Sumrall just stared at me, and that minute seemed like an eternity. He didn't answer, but rather put his fork down and stared… *at me.* Man, he had piercing eyes. He could look right through you.

Then he said, "You find the answer for missions right there in the Bible. Every seed reproduces after its own kind. There are two kinds of missions: There are those that send them and there are those that go and do it." Then he said, "You're the kind that go and do it. You'll have to go do it." That's how he talked. He was real blunt and plain. I fell in love with him that day. He was a great guy.

After that, we started missions. Because of that word, the following year in July of 1988, the Lord told me to go to Ireland. I bought a ticket on December the ninth and went to Dublin. The Irish Catholic-Protestant War was going on. It was a seemingly crazy move on my part, in retrospect, to go over there at that time and to do so alone, but when you're young and eager like I was, you just obey God.

While in Ireland, I went to scout out the land. One of my most memorable times in Ireland was when I preached from Mark, chapter 4, on the parable of the sower. I was preaching to a group of Catholics, and all of them came under the glory of God. It was quite impactful. From that one meeting, an outreach grew that culminated just last month in the dedication of a new twenty million dollar church in Dublin. It's the largest church in the entire nation, state-of-the art and gorgeous.

I've been doing missions in the Emerald Isle for twenty years. There were some violent times. There were threats made and even a bomb was set off near a place called Black Rock where I was speaking. Other than that, we've been very fortunate. We ministered outdoors on the streets. We set up tents. We preached in hotels. Eventually we started developing some strong ministers. We'd have them come over here to attend Bible school, get them through school, supply them with materials, and send them back home. We've put millions of dollars into missions in Ireland over the years, having been privileged to develop the three largest non-Catholic churches in the whole country. One of our students went back to Ireland and started his own church in Gallway called Abundant Life Gallway. It's a great church and a growing church on the West Coast right now.

I remember one time telling Dr. Sumrall that I was going to Ireland. I said, "I have some projects going on over in Ireland now."

His response was, "Man, I went to Ireland one time. I went over there and I ministered somewhere, and as I was leaving, these guys beat me up. I won't go back to Ireland. I'm glad it's you and not me." He said, "These guys, they had sticks or something, and because I was an American, they didn't like it that I was preaching. They beat me up pretty bad."

Because of Dr. Sumrall's faithfulness to deliver God's word to me that day, God has used our church mightily in assisting Ireland with His work. There were 248 people in the service the night Dr. Sumrall spoke at our first big conference. We have held an annual conference every year since then, and now thousands of people attend.

TV—I WAS SHAKING...I WAS SO NERVOUS

I shared earlier that I sang on live radio with my dad and mom on Sunday mornings when I was just six years old. Of the twenty years my parents did this, I assisted them for many years.

Once more, hindsight provided the answer to a *why*—as in, *Why did God have me go through certain experiences in my life?* I saw that doing live radio growing up had helped me prepare to go on television as an adult.

Our area didn't have a TV station. The closest one was in Houston. But we did have a small cable network where we were, and I contracted with them to film sessions of me teaching and preaching from our church auditorium. However, I was so intimidated by the very thought of doing this that I wouldn't do it on a Sunday morning. I asked the filming crew to come in on Monday when it would just be me without anyone else around.

I was wrestling with myself over doing this TV thing. I thought, *Why in the world am I doing this? I'm just starting this church up. I have a lot going on already, and now I am trying to do TV? Have I lost my mind?*

Nevertheless, I had the crew come over on a Monday. I planned to teach from Matthew, chapter 9, on the woman with the issue of blood. It was a scaled-down TV set up, with just one camera and a recorder; but, even at that, I found it overwhelming. Everything was put in place and I started speaking…and I was shaking. When that little red camera light came on, I was so nervous. My facial expressions and my actions all showed it.

I was sharing, "There was a little woman with an issue of blood." That's how it was coming out and I was thinking, *This is not my style!* I asked the camera man to stop filming. I said, "Just stop. I'm sorry." I came down off the small stage and went into my office. I got down on my knees there by my desk and started praying, saying, "God, You know that I said I'll do anything that You want me to do, but You're going to have to baptize me with 'boldness' to do this, because I can't stand it." It was more than I could handle all by myself.

I remained in my office for a while, praying to God like this in English and then praying in the Spirit, a key for victory in life. When I returned to the stage, something had changed in me, and for approximately thirty minutes, I delivered my message. When I was through, the cameraman gave his life to the Lord. He and I were the only ones there, and he asked Jesus into His life. I believe the experience of leading this man to the Lord meant that I was supposed to be on television. For about twenty years, I've been doing programs on TBN, then Daystar, and then on the GOD Channel when it first started over in Europe.

A GRIEVING FAMILY AND CHURCH

Following Angela's accident in 2002, I pulled away from TV. I felt that the Lord wanted my family—my wife, my two daughters, and me—to stay stable through all of this. I was especially concerned for my wife and my daughters, because it is difficult to anticipate how someone is going to deal with grief. I'll share more about this in pages to come.

We have always been a very close family. We have been in ministry together. None of my daughters has ever given me one day's trouble. They were a joy growing up. Our daughters have been accomplished musicians, public speakers, educated...*and pure.* They've always lived for God. All three are attractive, and boys have never been an issue. There was always a line of boys, but my daughters were cool about it. They figured they were going to get their choice one day, so they waited.

Angela was in her second semester in college and just two weeks from turning eighteen at the time of the accident. She commuted back and forth between college and home, and worked full-time for me. She was also a junior high youth pastor in our church.

When she died, I was very concerned how that was going to affect our family; and I had to consider the church as well. My church grieved right along with us; they love their pastor and his family. Many of them have been with us for eighteen years, and a large percentage of them got saved in my ministry. Not only were we grieving over Angela's death, but we were grieving over the deaths of two other people who died in the plane crash, amazing men of God from our church. Having never experienced anything like this, I didn't know what to anticipate, and I really didn't know who to turn to to tell me what to expect at this desperate time.

My concern, as I already stated, was especially for my family. People who are faced with tragedy don't always know if they're going to snap. Jumping off a roof can seem inviting as a way to deal with unbearable situations, yet Christians especially have an advantage when they're going through traumatic times. Still, I didn't want to leave the side of my wife and daughters. I was concerned that something would go badly for them, so I became ultra-protective of both my family and the church.

On top of this, we are a faith crowd. There are those who believe that if something bad happens, then there has to be something wrong—like sin in one's life—and God is judging that individual. *Yeah, this must have been God. Surely there was some sin in your life (or some wrongdoing on your part).* That kind of criticism was going on with some of our critics, very ignorant people.

Sin can open the door for bad things to happen, but it certainly isn't always the reason for these kinds of occurrences. It certainly wasn't the reason in our situation. I've been very blessed in that respect, in that I didn't have any guilt—not in my relationship with my wife or in raising my daughters. I had no regrets. I was able to go through my family's tragedy in grace and without regrets. People who have guilt have a terrible time getting through horrible situations. It affects them enormously. In hindsight, I can see that people who harbor guilt are easy targets for negative emotional addictions. Grief can become just that—a negative emotional addiction. I will deal with negative emotional addictions as they relate to grief in pages to come.

A BALM IN GILEAD

In dealing with Angela's death and all its ramifications, I pulled back on everything I did other than preach in the church. I shut down my ministerial organization which had almost a thousand ministers worldwide, and I stopped doing almost all television.

When my wife and I were hurting so badly, we would go upstairs to our big game room. I would take her by the arm; and we would start walking back and forth, back and forth. For long periods of time, we would cry, talk to God, and pray in the Spirit until the grief would lift and we would find the strength to function and continue forward one more day.

The pain is so deep when you lose a child. I have heard that it's the number one emotional trauma that can be experienced, the loss of a child, the premature death of a child. I don't know how this is determined; all I can say is that it was our worst nightmare. The suffering was unimaginable, but there is a "balm in Gilead" (Jeremiah 8:22), both a medicine and a Physician for applying healing ointment to the soul. There is a balm of sovereign capacity for healing the most desperate emotional and spiritual wounds. There is a Doctor in the house—if one is willing to receive. The pain is not from God, but the balm is.

There was no prayer in the natural that my wife and I could pray. No English words would do. Nothing of that sort would work. We couldn't ask God to heal Angela and bring her back. It was all beyond prayer that we could understand, so we prayed in the Spirit. That was part of our balm in Gilead.

> *Likewise the Spirit also helps in our weaknesses. For we do not know what we should pray for as we ought, but the Spirit Himself makes intercession for us with groanings which cannot be uttered...because He makes intercession for the saints according to the will of God.*
>
> *Romans 8:26-27* NKJV

> *For if I pray in a tongue, my spirit prays, but my understanding is unfruitful.*
>
> *1 Corinthians 14:14* NKJV

We just prayed in the Spirit, one of the most important things a child of God can do, especially at a time like this. Healing began to come. An oil of gladness was granted. We never broke out in hilarious laughing. Thank God when folks have been able to experience that, but it didn't happen for us. The oil of joy that we did experience managed to make us strong enough to get by. I never missed a message in my pulpit; I preached every one. Some of them were surely the worst messages I have ever preached in my life, but I preached them anyway. I was not going to let the devil get another victory in all of this. *I was not.*

Chapter 2

TELL MY DADDY IT DIDN'T HURT

As the twin-engine Cessna 340A started to crash into a vacant home in Temple, Texas, on January 17, 2002, my daughter Angela began praying in the Spirit. *The Daily News*, in its article, "Thousands Mourn Death of Pastor Killed in Plane Crash," said in regard to Angela's accident, "It was the image of the young evangelist speaking to God in a spiritual voice, even while facing death, that changed many tears of sorrow into shouts of praise Monday as thousands poured into Abundant Life Christian Center to say goodbye."

FILLED WITH VIRTUE AND ZEST, AHEAD OF HER AGE

In another article in *The Texas City Sun*, it was said of her, "Young Hallam laid to rest; recalled as virtuous and devoted to God.... The teen-age daughter of a La Marque pastor was remembered Monday as the church performer who lived a life filled with virtue and zest.... 'Angela Hallam lived an abundant life,' said Hassan Boyle, an Irish preacher...'She had peace and happiness. God was glorified in her.'"

Two others from our church were killed in that plane crash, and two were injured. Along with Angela, they were on their way to learn more about a youth ministry in Killeen, Texas.

My daughter's two-hour Homegoing Celebration began with a video tribute of her life from early childhood ballerina to a recent preaching engagement. "There is nothing better in the world than serving Jesus," she told the young people during a videotaped crusade.

I officiated at my daughter's funeral and, without the slightest reservation, encouraged those present to live for Jesus, telling them that my wife and I "have no regrets in raising our children to live for God."

Angela was our second child. When she was still a toddler, I followed the call of God on my life and began a church in our family's living room with ten founding members. As my ministry grew and took me around the world, Angela was often with me. She would observe and listen to the cream of the crop when it came to national and international speakers. She was making her own mental notes, storing up her own ideas for ministry.

At only seventeen, full of passion and ideas, she had already galvanized the junior high youth ministry as its pastor at our four thousand member church. It was always over the top. She was always thinking, *What can we do that's a little more? What can we do that shows a little bit more effort, a little bit more creativity?* Her life seemed to always rush ahead of her age. In a television interview at the time of the accident, one of the youth in our church said that Angela "did more in her life than many people have done through eighty years."

My daughter graduated from Abundant Life Christian School in May 2001—a year early and with honors—and was third in her class. She had a near-photographic memory, was active in the drama club— even voted "Most Dramatic"—received the Principal's Award, was a lady-in-waiting on the Homecoming Court, and was awarded best offensive player in All-State and All-District volleyball competition.

Her list of church activities was just as full: junior high youth pastor, praise and worship team, choir, and church drama. She had received national honors in drama through Oral Roberts University's Christian School Association competition—where, again, she was voted "Most Dramatic"—and won first-place in monologue and one-act dialogue.

Obviously Angela had both talent and passion for drama and theater. She had most recently organized "Heartbreak Hotel, Hotel Hallelujah," a live extravaganza featuring celebrity impersonators, animals, and bands. From February to April of the year before she went home, over 30,000 people—more than double the town's population—attended this stage production at our church. Some 3,000 committed their lives to Jesus Christ as a result.

I believe her generation is the greatest ever, and I believe she was proof of that.

I HAVE TO GO NOW

It was the day after Angela's accident. I was sitting in my car in the funeral home parking lot, bracing myself to go in and see my daughter. I had already identified her body the day before in Temple, Texas, the town where the plane crashed. I was like a lump of jelly, all wobbly and unsteady on the inside. God was all that was holding me together...mentally, emotionally, and physically. Struggling for a logical connection in all of this, for coherence of some kind, I was desperately thinking, *Man, how in the world am I going to get out of this car?* Then I received a telephone call.

It was one of my dear friends, a powerful minister from Colorado Springs. He said, "Walter." He was just sobbing and weeping on the phone as he called me. He said, "I saw Angela last night. *I saw her!*"

I asked, "What did you see?" because I would have given anything to see her. To this day, over eight years later, I haven't had even one dream about Angela. Maybe one day God will let me see her. Dr. Oral Roberts told me that He would. He said, "God will let you visit them [your loved ones who have gone on] in dreams and visions sometimes." He told me that this happened to him when he saw his daughter who had died in a plane crash.

This friend of mine told me, "I saw your daughter in heaven. I saw Angela in heaven." He said, "I almost never have dreams like this. But I had a dream, and I saw her; and it was so real. She was walking away from me with a lot of little children all around her. There were children all around her." Angela absolutely loved kids and was loved by them. She had devoted her life to connecting with kids.

My friend continued, "They were playing in a field at the time. And Angela stopped; and she turned around and said, *'This is my ministry. Children who have died and come to heaven prematurely—I teach them and train them about God and about the things of the kingdom. They don't know about it.'*"

Then my friend stated that Angela "Turned around and said, *'I have to go now. I have to go over there. I have to go over there with the kids.'* And she pointed to these kids who were all kind of running. She turned around as she was walking off, then she said to me, *'Tell my daddy it didn't hurt. Tell my daddy I just stepped in. It didn't hurt like that.'*"

It was a great word, very prophetic, and especially powerful because I knew Angela went to heaven instantly. There was a strong presence of God's anointing when my friend shared Angela's message for me. What a blessing. I have held so very tightly onto those words ever since.

At the time, sitting in the parking lot outside the funeral home, I didn't know all of the details of the last minutes before the plane crashed. These details gave further credence to Angela's words: *Tell my daddy it didn't hurt.* Weeks later, one of the survivors shared something of great import to me and my family about the accident.

She Stepped Out of Her Body... and Stepped In

Along with the senior youth pastor and senior pilot, there were two youth ministry interns on the plane with Angela. Only the two interns survived.

Angela had been sitting there with her Bible in her lap. The pilot told the passengers that they were experiencing difficulty. The plane began to descend in a glide toward a subdivision, and was soon to crash into a vacant house. Angela was really aggressive when it came to prayer. She was very mature for her age, spiritually and otherwise. Later, one of the interns shared with me all the details of what happened right before the plane crash. He said, "She was praying really loudly. And then I didn't hear her. We were all praying very intensely in the back of the plane there. I turned and looked because Angela had stopped praying. She was just slumped in the chair. And then moments later, there was the impact; and they were all gone."

My friend had told me that Angela said, *Tell my daddy it didn't hurt. Tell my daddy I just stepped in. It didn't hurt like that.* I totally believe that she actually stepped out of her body before the plane crashed.

So when I think about the accident now, I refuse to look at the negative. Rather, I rejoice over heaven's gain. When I had identified my daughter at the hospital the night before, I could tell that she had taken a hard hit on her head; but, other than that, she had hardly any marks on her. She must have hit the bulkhead of the plane. The two interns, who were in the back with Angela, were knocked unconscious. Two other wonderful men—the pilot and my youth pastor—and Angela went to heaven instantly. They stepped into heaven that day.

Chapter 3

REVELATION AND INFORMATION

The Big Why is not just good teaching from the Word of God, with nice sequential steps and the perfect Scriptures put perfectly in place to support each step. It goes beyond teaching, beyond acquiring knowledge. Knowledge will often take one no further than logical reasoning.

FAITH AND LOGIC

Logical reasoning has its place in the life of the believer, but it must be kept in its place. The Bible says that "the just shall live by faith" (Hebrews 10:38). When it comes to faith, we must recognize that faith and logic do not always get along. Logic can conflict with many of the Bible's teaching such as giving in order to receive, or dying in order to live, or being last in order to be first, or being a servant in order to be great...or leaving ninety-nine sheep in order to rescue one. (Luke 15:3-7.) The logical mind says the shepherd is taking too big a risk in leaving ninety-nine sheep to go after the one that is lost. That doesn't logically compute until we—you and I—are the one lost sheep. Then it makes a lot of sense!

Exercising our faith does not require us to reject sound reasoning. The truth is that the God-kind of faith does not go against reason, but rather goes *beyond* it. Faith doesn't go *around* reason or circumvent it and then run ahead. It *includes* reason and contains it as a subordinate element but then rises above it and transcends it into something of more worth and deeper understanding.

Our mind is a valuable asset to God if it is yielded to God. We simply must not let our intellectual reasoning overrule the voice of God. When it comes to God's ways and thoughts, Isaiah 55:9 tells us: "For as the heavens are higher than the earth, so are my ways higher than your ways, and my thoughts than your thoughts." God is not telling us that our ways and thoughts are of no value to Him. He is simply saying that His ways and thoughts are higher than ours, exceeding ours. I further believe that He wants us to strive to know His higher ways and higher thoughts.

It is important to point out that *The Big Why* goes beyond information and mere intellectual reasoning, but not against them. It is revelatory. Information is good. Intellectual reasoning is good. But revelation is another matter…it's the only place where some of the why's get answered.

In revelation, we find an understanding of the wisdom of God that the natural man cannot acquire through information and reasoning alone. (1 Corinthians 2:7.)

> *But as it is written, Eye hath not seen, nor ear heard, neither have entered into the heart of man, the things which God hath prepared for them that love him.*
>
> *But God hath revealed them unto us by his Spirit: for the Spirit searcheth all things, yea, the deep things of God.*
>
> *For what man knoweth the things of a man, save the spirit of man which is in him? even so the things of God knoweth no man, but the Spirit of God.*

Now we have received, not the spirit of the world, but the spirit which is of God; that we might know the things that are freely given to us of God.

But the natural man receiveth not the things of the Spirit of God: for they are foolishness unto him: neither can he know them, because they are spiritually discerned.

1 Corinthians 2:9-12,14

Some things we'll never know—I don't care who we are in life and how much experience or education we have. There are some things we'll never know unless God reveals them to us. There are some things that neither eyes nor ears will reveal, "but God hath revealed them unto us by his Spirit" (1 Corinthians 2:10). We know what we know by *experience* or *learning,* or by *revelation,* but there is an unseen realm. There is an unseen world, and God will allow us to see or understand it many times through the Word of God and the Spirit of God.

THE WORD AND THE SPIRIT

Notice I stated, "through the Word of God and the Spirit of God." It takes both. Some people want to cling to the Spirit and de-emphasize the Word; others want to cling to the Word and de-emphasize the Holy Spirit. Some say that they just go by the Holy Spirit—"I'm just led by the Spirit." Well, certainly, we are supposed to be led by the Spirit of God. "For as many as are led by the Spirit of God, they are the sons of God" (Romans 8:14). The question becomes: how can we know that we're truly being led by the Spirit of God, if we don't know the Word? It is the Word that the Spirit will confirm. Mark 16:20 tells us that the Lord worked with His disciples and confirmed *His Word* through manifestations of the Spirit. It is gravely dangerous to have the Spirit without the Word.

Then there are those who are proud sticklers of the Word, but fail to realize that it's possible to find a Bible verse to support almost anything that someone wants to believe or do. Scriptures can be twisted: misinterpreted, taken out of context, or not put in context with other Scriptures dealing with the same matter. We are told:

> *For precept must be upon precept, precept upon precept; line upon line, line upon line; here a little, and there a little.*
>
> *Isaiah 28:10*

> *In the mouth of two or three witnesses shall every word be established.*
>
> *2 Corinthians 13:1*

Speaking of two or three witnesses, a word of Scripture should line up with what the Holy Spirit says in our spirit; otherwise we're playing the dangerous game of having the Word without the Spirit. The Word and the Spirit, together, should agree.

> *And it is the Spirit that beareth witness, because the Spirit is truth.*
>
> *1 John 5:6*

> *And there are three that bear witness in earth, the Spirit, and the water, and the blood: and these three agree in one.*
>
> *1 John 5:8*

Jesus, the Word of God made flesh, "came by water and blood" (1 John 5:6). 1 John 5:8 tells us, in essence, that the Word and the Spirit agree.

God is a Spirit: and they that worship him must worship him in spirit and in truth.

John 4:24

Our spirit and the Holy Spirit on the inside, together, are involved in the pursuit of truth. We can't depend on intellect alone, because the mind does not know all things.

What many have failed to realize is that there is a difference between the letter of the Word and the Word of the Spirit which Jesus says, "The words that I speak unto you, they are spirit, and they are life" (John 6:63). We have been made ministers, "not of the letter but of the Spirit; for the letter kills, but the Spirit gives life" (2 Corinthians 3:6 NKJV). The Spirit of the living God is instilled into the letter of the Word, causing it to become more than a written code. It becomes "living and powerful...piercing...and is a discerner" (Hebrews 4:12 NKJV). We cannot separate the Word from the Spirit and the Spirit from the Word. *We must have both!*

We know what we know by *experience, learning,* or by *revelation.* Yet there is an unseen world, and many times God will allow us to see it through the Word of God *and* the Spirit of God.

THE SPIRITUAL AND THE NATURAL

All experience has a degree of revelation within it. With the benefit of hindsight, a lot of why's can be answered if we grasp the spiritual revelation that goes with an experience.

There is a difference between intellectual knowledge and experiential learning. We could call intellectual knowledge *science-lab learning,* as in a mere "mind-quest" for information. The science lab is an artificial environment. Science lab learning deals with hypothetical situations, selected variables, experimentation, and theories of cause and effect. This is different from the learning that takes place with real people and real, believable situations. In the context of real life, we don't have the option of testing several hypothetical situations and inserting different variables of our choice, before narrowing it all down to the situation that makes us the most comfortable. We don't always get to choose between door number one or door number two, hypothetical situation number one or hypothetical situation number two.

As Christians within the providence of God, we have been given power to create our own reality through our thoughts—"For as he [a man] thinketh in his heart, so is he" (Proverbs 23:7)—and through our confessions—"Death and life are in the power of the tongue" (Proverbs 18:21). We also live in a world where the sun rises "on the evil and on the good" and rain falls "on the just and on the unjust" (Matthew 5:45). Real-life experiences can give us revelatory knowledge better than science lab learning.

Information is good and will give us a lot of strength, but it won't answer all our questions. With the blessing of hindsight, we can understand a lot of things if we're willing, because hindsight has a spiritual side that explains the *why*. If everything has to be defined only in black and white, there are some questions that will never be answered. If we're able to embrace both the spiritual and the natural, then we can understand even the most difficult inquiries.

In the Book of Daniel, King Belshazzar was desperate to find someone who could read and interpret the handwriting on the wall. The queen told King Belshazzar about Daniel:

REVELATION AND INFORMATION

There is a man in thy kingdom, in whom is the spirit of the
holy gods; and in the days of thy father light and understanding
and wisdom, like the wisdom of the gods, was found in
him…Forasmuch as an excellent spirit, and knowledge, and
understanding, interpreting of dreams, and shewing of hard
sentences, and dissolving of doubts, were found in the same
Daniel….

Daniel 5:11-12

"Understanding…and shewing of hard sentences"—the New King James Version translates this as "solving riddles, and explaining enigmas." In other words, Daniel was a man of understanding who could explain difficult situations; he wouldn't just give "pat" answers. The world doesn't want pat answers—readily and easily spoken, but unconvincing, without a lot of thought, shallow, having to do with what is apparent but not necessarily real. Today, this young generation will quickly be turned off over a pat answer *because they're smart.* They live in a world where much information is available, and they want answers to the hard questions. They want the solutions to difficult problems, not just the easy ones. They are looking for the "dissolving of doubts" (v. 12).

Much of what has been called unexplainable is explainable. Jesus visited me in a very spiritual experience forty days after the death of my daughter. He encouraged me and instructed me, revealing scriptural reasons behind the tragedies and challenges of life. Through these startling biblical revelations, I learned some of the invaluable *why's* of life, and what we can do to prevent future loss. It was instruction from heaven. When Jesus speaks, remember, "The words that I [Jesus] speak unto you, they are *spirit*, and they are *life*" (John 6:63). They are alive and full of power.

I believe that before something of God manifests in the natural realm, it takes place first in the spiritual realm. The role of the Church is to be God's instrument to bring what He has already done in the spiritual realm into the physical world, in a tangible way. I believe *The Big Why* has a role to play in assisting this process.

PART TWO

THE
FIRST
VISITATION

AN UNJUST WEIGHT

Forty days had passed since Angela's plane crash, and I still had not received a word from God—at least, not directly—in relation to the accident. My wife and I had been praying a lot, just trying to survive. It had been horrible. I did not understand, and I just didn't know what to do. Cindy and I were desperate.

It was very late, and I was sound asleep, only to be awakened in the middle of the night. I have a digital clock that I can easily see on the table next to my bed. I turned my head to see that it was 3:22 A.M. This is significant because 3:22 in the afternoon was the exact time of Angela's plane crash. It's like Jesus was making a point that He was fully aware of the crime that took place that day and that He was keeping record of it all. Before the night was to end, I would be awakened 2 more times: —once at 4:22 and again at 6:22.

Somebody was standing beside me—a figure about six feet tall. I could see the features of His face only somewhat; they were not really clear, but somehow I knew I was in the presence of the Lord. This awareness left me lying there in a near-paralytic state.

He spoke to me. The very first words to come out of His mouth were: "I know exactly how you feel. I lost three of my top leaders, and it was unjust." That's exactly what He said, and just like that—forthright and sober. "I lost John the Baptist," He continued, "I lost James the brother of John, and I lost Stephen. And it was unjust."

Until that night, I honestly had no comprehension of the true gravity of the message in Proverbs 11:1—"A false balance is abomination to the LORD; but a just weight is his delight." Plain and simple, it is saying that an *unjust weight is an abomination to God.*

The Hebrew word for *balance* implies a survey instrument or scale. In Bible days, if someone brought in some gold bullion to determine its quantity, he would put it on a scale. A known weight would be used to counterbalance the scale such as stones, to determine the exact weight of the gold bullion. If an unjust weight was used, it was for the intent of tricking the customer. Such practice is called an "abomination" in the Word of God. The word *abomination* in Proverbs 11:1 implies something repugnantly hateful, detestable, and loathsome, greatly disliked, or abhorred; a vile, shameful action.

The false balance in Proverbs 11:1 is symbolic of unjust and fraudulent dealings with anyone. All of these dealings, according to this verse, are an *abomination* to the Lord. They go beyond being a mere affront to justice, beyond being merely offensive—they are abominable. God Himself is the patron—the supporter and protector—of justice, which includes being the supporter and protector of the wronged individual. He is the avenger of those who are defrauded.

Chapter 4

UNDERSTANDING
THE SOVEREIGNTY OF GOD

Before going any further with *The Big Why*, we need to discuss the sovereignty of God. There are those who will question right away, "Where is God when people are being treated unjustly? Doesn't He see everything? Isn't God in control of everything; and, therefore, nothing can happen unless He allows it to happen? After all, He's God; He can do anything!"

Not only is there a hurting world in dire need of understanding along this line, but there is a Church in need of this understanding, as well. First of all, God is not in control of *everything*. It is not a matter of Him *allowing* all that happens to happen. God will not do *just anything*. Because we have misunderstood this, God has been blamed for many things that He had nothing to do with. Moreover, His created beings have resigned themselves to doing nothing about things they should be resisting, attacking, or even that they are causing to happen. After all, if God is sanctioning something, why should we resist or attack it or try to cause something else to take place? Please, before anyone jumps to any wrong conclusions or gets offended by what I have just stated, let me explain.

A Matter of Semantics

When it comes to teaching and preaching about God and the things of God, too often we fail to clearly define the terms we have used. It's a matter of semantics or word meanings. For example, we have talked about *dying to the flesh* without explaining what we mean by "the flesh." We have talked about *crucifying self*, without making it clear what we are referring to by "self." We have talked about *coming out from the world* and being a separate people, but we haven't made it clear what we mean by "the world." What's happened as a result, is that we have too often "thrown the baby out with the bath water," to use a familiar expression.

We have killed good, God-given desires along with the bad ones. We have snuffed out destinies and failed to use God-given talents, while cocooning ourselves in our cozy, little Christian environments. We've insulated ourselves from a world that has desperately needed us—particularly the God Who is inside us. So, when it comes to talking about God Himself, we have misunderstood the sovereignty of God and have done a lot of speculating about Him that has been in error.

Now I will repeat what I stated earlier: first of all, God is not in control of everything. It is not a matter of Him *allowing* all that happens to happen. God will not do *just anything*. Because we have misunderstood this, God has been blamed for many things that He had nothing to do with.

I have heard statements such as: "Anything that has happened is in God's timing. Everything is by His design. We can rejoice in the fact that God is in control of our lives." While these statements might "preach" well, I beg to differ.

God chose to not be in control of everything when He chose to make man in His own image. This means that man was endowed with some of God's own attributes—not the least of which is free will. God gave man a will, and the freedom to make his own choices.

On the one hand, God gave humans the free will to choose, and He will not violate the will He gave us. On the other hand, demons and those they work through, love to violate both God's will and the human will. God gives us the freedom to choose and, as Titus 1:2 points out, He is the God "that cannot lie." "It was impossible for God to lie," Hebrews 6:18 says. God will not go against His Word. To do so would make Him no longer the God of the Bible. It would go against His very nature.

TREASURE IN EARTHEN VESSELS

Does this in any way diminish the omnipotence and omniscience of God? Was it a stupid move on God's part to give man this kind of leverage? Leverage implies power or ability to act or to influence people, events, or decisions. God's Word tells us, "Thou madest him to have dominion over the works of thy hands; thou hast put all things under his feet" (Psalm 8:6). Only a God of the greatest strength and wisdom would not be threatened by putting His "treasure in earthen vessels" (2 Corinthians 4:7). Only a God of the utmost strength and wisdom would dare to create a people in His search for a family—a people who, out of His love for them, would be His portion, and who, out of their love for Him, would choose Him to be theirs. They would *choose* to say, "God, I love you." They would *choose* to obey Him. This made for *real* people and a *real* relationship.

God wanted to have the joy of fellowshipping with man. His other creatures—the birds, the fish, and the beasts—do not have a will, but go by instinct. They go by their innate impulses rather than willful, voluntary obedience to God, but man's obedience is a matter of choice. With obedience comes the possibility of disobedience. Somehow in the scheme of things, *God found us to be worth the risk.* This revelation alone should put wind beneath our wings.

When Adam and Eve failed to obey, it was a God of the utmost wisdom and strength who, rather than protect His reputation, has been more interested in redeeming and restoring human beings. Satan wants to make God regret this decision and think it was the greatest mistake of His eternal lifetime. God's Word, the Bible, is the most widely-published book of all times, with a far greater circulation than any book around today. Yet God saw fit to publish in this very book Abraham's doubting Him, taking on a Hagar, fathering an Ishmael—with the end result being the turmoil that is now going on in the Middle East. God shared in His Word the instance of Noah's drunkenness, Samson's fornication, David's murderous and adulterous acts, and Peter's denial. The list goes on and on.

In sharing His divine plan, not only the good but the faults, shortcomings, and even sins of His people, God made Himself vulnerable to scrutiny, attack, and ridicule. There were those who would use God's honesty and transparency as ammunition to shoot down His very worthiness, appeal, and power which should have kept His own people strong and on the right path.

God was and continues to be interested in redeeming and restoring human beings. He is more interested in us than He is in protecting His own reputation. Ultimately, His reputation will protect itself. God has revealed the shortcomings of His creation; He hasn't shoved under the carpet the failures and sins of His people. He is more interested in our acquiring understanding and in changing patterns of wrong behavior. *He is more interested in us!* God saw the value of revealing people's choices and actions and the corresponding consequences so that we could learn from others' mistakes.

The bottom line is: He saw the value in us and, even more, He loved us to the extent that He wanted us to be His family forever. This includes sharing His eternal life, His power, and His creation. For this to happen, He had to send His own Son to be the perfect sacrifice, because our sins had separated us from Him. He dared and continues to dare to love us. Before it is all over, this love will mark Him as a God of the utmost wisdom and strength. He will have a people—a family, "a great multitude, which no man could number, of all nations, and kindreds, and people, and tongues" (Revelation 7:9)—for all eternity. Satan, shall "be brought down to hell, to the sides of the pit" (Isaiah 14:15).

Was it a mistake for God to give man free will? Does this in anyway diminish the omnipotence and omniscience of God? Was this a stupid move on God's part to give man this kind of leverage in the scheme of things? My answer to these questions is, *I don't think so; I truly don't think so.* "What is man, that thou art mindful of him? and the son of man, that thou visitest him?" (Psalm 8:4). I only have to consider my daughter Angela to say, *God, You knew what You were doing.*

We see the theme of man's freedom of choice throughout the Bible, beginning in the Garden of Eden. Man could choose to obey God's command to not eat of the tree of the knowledge of good and evil, but he didn't! (Genesis 2:17.) There are other examples, too numerous to list them all, but here are a few:

...I have set before you life and death, blessing and cursing: therefore choose...

Deuteronomy 30:19

And if it seem evil unto you to serve the LORD, choose you this day whom ye will serve...

Joshua 24:15

And Elijah came unto all the people, and said, How long halt ye between two opinions? If the LORD be God, follow him: but if Baal, then follow him...

1 Kings 18:21

Know ye not, that to whom ye yield yourselves servants to obey, his servants ye are to whom ye obey; whether of sin unto death, or of obedience unto righteousness.

Romans 6:16

THWARTING THE PLAN OF GOD

It is God's will that none "should perish, but that all should come to repentance" (2 Peter 3:9), but multitudes of souls will not choose to do this. If God had His way, no one would go to hell; but God is not getting His way—not in this regard. God created every human being with a plan in mind—"For I know the thoughts and plans that I have for you" (Jeremiah 29:11 AMP). However, because God gave human beings a free will, they can choose not to recognize God's plan for their lives. They can spend all of their lives out of the will of God, circumventing God's plan for them, doing their own thing.

People's sins, foolishness, and ignorance can temporarily and even eternally thwart the plan of God for their lives. As believers, we are part of this family of mankind, and can be affected by the sins, foolishness, and ignorance of others. That can thwart the plan of God in our own life on a temporary basis. Let's get real: The lives of godly parents are affected by the ungodly behavior of their children, and vice versa. The ungodly behavior of siblings, neighbors, and fellow employees, can affect our lives. Psalm 105 tells us that Joseph was "sold for a servant" (v. 17)—an act committed by his own brothers—"Whose feet they hurt with fetters: he was laid in iron" (v. 18). Joseph *felt* the pain; this was no walk in the park.

Because we are interconnected in this great scheme of things, other people affect the plan of God for our lives and we affect the plan of God for their lives. We hold keys for each other, such as love, encouragement, support, information, wisdom, and finances. Sometimes people do not come through for us as they should, and, of course, we don't always come through for others as we should. Sometimes someone drops us—like Mephibosheth, the son of Jonathan, who was dropped and left crippled when his nurse was running from the enemy's army. (2 Samuel 4:4.) We've been dropped! Does that mean that God allowed it—since He's omnipotent and did not step in to stop it? Does that mean that God was in control of this? Does that mean that this was in God's timing? *No!*

If our hearts are right before God, He can still make a way for us in the midst of such affectation. Things *will* work together for our good. (Romans 8:28.) What the enemy meant for evil, God *will* use it for good. (Genesis 50:20.)

ULTIMATELY GOD HAS HIS WAY

God has a plan for every human being, yet men can spend all their lives circumventing that plan. There is one part of God's plan that they will not be able to circumvent. The time will come when they will have to give an accounting to God for what they have done with what He has entrusted them with. They will either spend eternity in heaven or hell, depending on whether they chose to live for God or against Him. Our God is a God of mercy and forgiveness, but we cannot leave out that He will indeed punish sin.

There are those who will scream: "I don't think God works like that; I don't feel like He does things that way." God doesn't go by how we think or feel; He goes by His Word, and His Word says,

> *For we must all appear before the judgment seat of Christ; that*
> *every one may receive the things done in his body, according to*
> *that he hath done, whether it be good or bad.*
> *2 Corinthians 5:10*

> *And Enoch also, the seventh from Adam, prophesied of these,*
> *saying, Behold, the Lord cometh with ten thousands of his saints,*
> *to execute judgment upon all, and to convince all that are ungodly*

among them of all their ungodly deeds which they have ungodly
committed, and of all their hard speeches which ungodly sinners
have spoken against him.

Jude 14-15

There are those who will say, "I don't believe all of this stuff about heaven or hell." They have a right to do that, because God gave them the right to choose. But just because they do not believe in this "stuff" doesn't make this "stuff" *false*. If something is true, not believing it doesn't make it false—it is true regardless. And vice versa: If something is false, all the sincere, well-intended, and intense believing in the world that it is true will not make it true—it is still false. We can be sincere, and be sincerely wrong. "Let God be true, but every man a liar" (Romans 3:4).

There are those who will assert, "I don't think that is right that I have to give an accounting to God." Not only does God reserve the right to demand such an accounting, we will see in the pages ahead that God reserves the right as the Universal Doctor of Jurisprudence to vindicate those who have been treated unjustly.

Chapter 5

I WILL RECOMPENSE

The Lord said to me in my bedroom that night, "An unjust weight is an abomination, and I'll repay it. I'll recompense." God said that He will recompense what was taken; He'll pay it back. Justice involves rewards for the righteous and judgment upon the unrighteous. For those righteous who have been victimized and robbed, God promises to recompense—to repay, to make restitution, to compensate for the injury or damage or wrong committed against them.

RECOMPENSING THE DEATHS OF JOHN, JAMES, AND STEPHEN

The Lord told me, "Go and look at what I was able to do because of the unjustness of those men's deaths," referring to John the Baptist, James, and Stephen. John the Baptist—"The voice of one crying in the wilderness, Prepare ye the way of the Lord, make his paths straight" (Matthew 3:3)—with his clothing of camel's hair, preached to Jerusalem, Judaea, and all around the area of Jordan, and baptized his converts in the River of Jordan. (Matthew 3:5,6.) God used John to set the stage for Jesus' ministry before he was beheaded by King Herod.

Later Herod decided to wreak some havoc and go after the Church by beheading James, the brother of the apostle John. (Acts 12:1-2.) The reaction over James' death sent Herod after Peter, whom he had arrested. While Peter was bound in chains, the Church gathered in prayer. The end result was that the angel of the Lord freed Peter from prison and churches were started that spread into Asia Minor. We can read about them in the book of Revelation.

Then there was Stephen, the third person Jesus referred to as one of His top leaders who was unjustly lost. No justifiable reason for Stephen's death can be found. "Full of faith and power" and doer of "great wonders and miracles among the people" (Acts 6:8), Stephen was tried by the Sanhedrin for blasphemy against Moses and God, and for speaking against the temple and the law (vv. 11,13-14). Prior to his trial, Acts 6:10 records: "And they were not able to resist the wisdom and the spirit by which he spake." During Stephen's trial, "All that sat in the council, looking stedfastly on him, saw his face as it had been the face of an angel" (Acts 6:15). Right before his execution, Stephen said, "Behold, I see the heavens opened, and the Son of man standing on the right hand of God" (Acts 7:56). Even while being executed, Stephen "kneeled down, and cried with a loud voice, Lord, lay not this sin to their charge. And when he had said this, he fell asleep" (Acts 7:60). Stephen was stoned to death by an enraged mob encouraged by Saul of Tarsus, the future Apostle Paul. However, because of his death, persecution of the Church drove its members "every where preaching the word" (Acts 8:1,4). God recompensed the deaths of John the Baptist, James, and Stephen. He made restitution for the loss the enemy caused.

A LEGAL DOOR OF ENTRY

God despises, abhors, and detests any unjust weight or any fraudulent actions aimed at His children. It is one thing when a robbery takes place when a legal door of entry is provided. It is quite another matter when the victim leaves no legal door of entry open.

Sometimes legal doors of entry are left open. Take, for example, a person who blatantly disobeys the law and ends up injured or dead. Driving above the speed limit can lead to a deadly accident. There are natural laws that govern the proper functioning and care of one's body. Abusing our bodies can result in disease or death. Our very words can set us up for victory or defeat.

A man's belly shall be satisfied with the fruit of his mouth; and with the increase of his lips shall he be filled. Death and life are in the power of the tongue: and they that love it shall eat the fruit thereof.

Proverbs 18:20-21

These examples show that both common sense and our words have a part to play in keeping the door of entry shut to the enemy. These things are under our control. It is a different situation when no such door has been opened for theft, accidents, disease, or even death.

No Legal Door of Entry

What about people whose lives were obviously intruded upon by the enemy, yet there was no blatant sin going on in their lives, no neglect, physical or spiritual, and no rebellion? What about people who were walking in obvious close relationship with the Father? What about people who were being used mightily in the work of the Lord, even at the height of their ministry?

This is what the Lord was addressing that night He came to visit me. There are times when the enemy will attack and he does not have a legal door of entry. No door has been opened through sin or anything else that would give the devil legal access to one's life. Then there are times when that unlawful entry is of such a violent, obtrusive nature that there is the spilling of blood—death. These are unjust weights where a different kind of recompense is required.

This was the case with John the Baptist, James, and Stephen. This was also the case with ten of the other apostles. (John, of course, died at an old age; and we've already discussed James, his brother, who was beheaded.) Christian tradition in general says that all of the other apostles were martyred, but the sources for specific details of their deaths are somewhat unreliable. Peter was crucified upside-down on his cross. Andrew, Philip, Jude, and Simon the Zealot were crucified, as well. Nathanael was skinned-alive and then beheaded. Matthew's death was administered by a shafted weapon with an axe-like cutting blade and spike. Thomas was killed by a spear. James, son of Alphaeus, was crucified, then stoned, then beaten to death with a club. Matthias was beheaded after being stoned.[1]

For centuries, even millennia, God's people have been martyred. We only have to look at Hebrews, chapter 11 for their stories. While there were those who received "their dead raised to life again,"

> ...others were tortured, not accepting deliverance; that they might obtain a better resurrection: and others had trial of cruel mockings and scourgings, yea, moreover of bonds and imprisonment: they were stoned, they were sawn asunder, were tempted, were slain with the sword: they wandered about in sheepskins and goatskins; being destitute, afflicted, tormented; (of whom the world was not worthy:) they wandered in deserts, and in mountains, and in dens and caves of the earth.
>
> Hebrews 11:35-38 (emphasis mine)

There is no indication that these men of God did anything that gave the devil a legal right to take their lives. Today's statistics for violent persecution of Christians are global and astonishing. There are Christians who suffer for their faith today, even to the point of death. They cannot be accused of opening the door to the enemy to come in and do such a thing. They cannot be accused of not knowing how to exercise their rights as children of God. What is being done to them by the adversary is a false balance, and it is an abomination to God. But just as the enemy did not get the last word when John the Baptist, James, Stephen and certain apostles were martyred, the enemy will not get the last word in his violent assault on the children of God today. History reveals that great moves of God follow atrocities, and we can expect great moves of God today.

The point that we must understand here is that God will recompense differently when a victim has been robbed, even of life, when there has been no door of entry opened by the victim. When there is unlawful invasion of the enemy, spilling of blood, or death there is a magnification of God's restoration and recompense.

RECOMPENSED IN THE EARTH

God promises to restore all that the enemy has taken. His divine justice promises to recompense blessings upon the righteous. While there is a final, ultimate judgment there is, as well, a promise of recompense here on the earth for the righteous. "The righteous shall be recompensed [or rewarded] in the earth," says Proverbs 11:31. I will share more about this when I talk about Jesus' third visitation and His promise to me that "their works do follow them" (Revelation 14:13), but for now, some powerful scriptural examples can give us a good idea of what Jesus was saying to me when He said, "I will recompense."

THE BIG WHY

Job's life was plundered by Satan. Of Job, the Lord Himself said, "Hast thou considered my servant Job, that there is none like him in the earth, a perfect and an upright man, one that feareth God, and escheweth evil?" (Job 1:8). Job abstained from evil; he shunned it. From what Scripture says, there is no sin to be detected in this man's life. Yet, Job suffered loss of property, health, friends, and, most significantly, his children. He experienced lack of sympathy, and his faith was stretched beyond imagination. However, in the end, the devil's onslaught brought about the Lord's recompense of "twice as much as he had before….So the LORD blessed the latter end of Job more than his beginning" (Job 42:10,12). The captivity of Job was turned around. (Job 42:10.)

Isaiah 61:7 says, "For your shame ye shall have double; and for confusion they shall rejoice in their portion: therefore in their land they shall posses the double: everlasting joy shall be unto them." I like how the Amplified Bible renders this: "Instead of your [former] shame you shall have a twofold recompense; instead of dishonor and reproach [your people] shall rejoice in their portion. Therefore in their land they shall possess double [what they had forfeited]; everlasting joy shall be theirs."

There is a difference between shame brought on by one's own sins, foolishness, or ignorance and shame that the enemy tries to inflict. The enemy will not only attempt to violently invade without just cause; he will also attempt to bring reproach upon the child of God. The devil will try to humiliate him, to point an accusing finger at him so that others blame him for the loss that's really the devil's doing.

In Job's case, the adversary tried to make it look like Job's suffering was punishment for his sin. Job's three accusers argued that it's possible to gauge God's favor or disfavor toward a person by examining his prosperity or lack thereof, or his adversities or lack thereof. Satan tried to confuse the real issue. He attempted to add insult to injury, to compound his atrocity by stacking shame on top of it. But his attempt to double the trouble only positioned God to double the honor for all the dishonor. Isaiah 50:7 tells us this: "For the Lord GOD will help me; therefore shall I not be confounded: therefore have I set my face like a flint, and I know that I shall not be ashamed." God recompenses and as it says in Isaiah 61:7, He promises a "twofold recompense."

We can't leave Joseph's story out here—Joseph who was "sold for a servant" (Psalm 105:17) by his own brothers. Joseph may have been foolish to share his two dreams with his brothers. In these dreams, God put him in a place of honor above his brothers, and they "hated him yet the more for his dreams, and for his words" (Genesis 37:8), and "envied him" (v. 11). But Joseph certainly did not give the devil a legal door of entry by the way he conducted himself before his masters as his conduct gave him grace and favor on more than one occasion.

His running from the seductive wife of one of his masters certainly gave no place to the enemy, yet for this he was thrown into prison. He did not deny the Lord even in prison. When Pharaoh's butler and baker asked him to interpret their dreams, Joseph responded, "Do not interpretations belong to God? tell me them, I pray you" (Genesis 40:8). This would have been the perfect opportunity for Joseph to say, "Interpretations belong to God, and does it look like God is with me? You've come to the wrong man to get your dreams interpreted." But he didn't; instead he interpreted the dreams, believing that even in the midst of his horrible circumstances that God *was* with him.

God recompensed for the enemy's unjust balance. "The king sent and loosed him [Joseph]; even the ruler of the people, and let him go free" (Psalm 105:20). Joseph didn't just go free; "He [the king, the pharaoh] made him lord of his house, and ruler of all his substance: to bind his princes at his pleasure; and teach his senators wisdom" (vv. 21-22). Sometimes the journey to our "between a rock and a hard place" is long and painful, but with God, the recovery can be swift—even overnight. The Spirit of God can do more in a second than we can do in a lifetime.

We have become so well-versed in the body of Christ in the five steps to receiving our healing, the four steps to hearing from God, the seven steps to getting delivered, and the six steps to becoming financially free. This can be good in that God wants to build our maturity and character through various steps so we can handle the blessings ahead. But sometimes we limit God by waiting for step two to follow step one and step four to follow step three. My experience has been that sometimes while we've been in the dungeon, enough character and maturity have been worked into us that we can skip some of the steps to our recovery. We are more ready for God's victory than we realize. We may skip steps that we and others are convinced will be necessary because God is able to work quickly in the days ahead in the lives of those who have been viciously and illegally attacked by the adversary.

When the enemy comes to steal where there has been no legal entry provided, he has to pay for that. This is especially true when he sheds innocent blood (as was the case with Job). "These six things doth the LORD hate: yea, seven are an abomination unto him: A proud look, a lying tongue, and *hands that shed innocent blood*" (Proverbs 6:16-17, emphasis mine). There's a different recompense that is due when innocent blood has been shed. The Lord spoke to me the night of His visitation, "You stay faithful during this time, this difficult time. I'm going to give you a double recompense the remaining days of your life."

Speaking of Satan trying to confuse the real issues, there are those who will get upset and call it "the devil" if it looks like God is blessing our life. Now that may surprise some, but it is true. I have often stated, "Don't ever judge a man's harvest till you examine his seed." I'll share a brief story along this line. As soon as I stepped off the plane in California recently for a ministry engagement, a pastor-friend of mine called. He said, "You're not going to believe what just happened."

I asked, "What just happened?"

He said, "I went to see a man the other day. I didn't know the man, but he wanted to meet me. I found out who he was, and I took the meeting. Actually, he came to see me. He came in, sat down in the office, and talked to me for a few minutes; and then he said, 'Well, I've got something for you.'"

That gentleman gave my friend three million dollars right there on the spot. Whew! I know for a fact that my pastor-friend is a big giver. I'll just repeat what I previously stated: Never judge a man's harvest until you examine his seed.

I've heard people criticize great men like Kenneth Copeland. I know Reverend Copeland; we've been friends for quite a few years. Every year he sows hundreds of thousands of dollars worth of money, planes, food, clothing, and other goods to the work of the Lord. He gives like that *every year*. Now, I know he *receives* a lot of money; but he *gives* a lot of money, as well. We must never judge a harvest until we examine the seed.

In my case, everything I am doing right now prospers. While I know that *trustworthiness* is part of the reason for this, there's a recompense in it, as well because of what the enemy came to unjustly take from me and my family. God gave me that revelation: *An unjust weight is an abomination and I'll repay it. I'll recompense.*

IN LEAGUE WITH GOD

"For I the Lord love justice; I hate robbery and wrong with violence…And I will faithfully give them their recompense in truth, and I will make an everlasting covenant or league with them" (Isaiah 61:8 AMP). God let me know that night that He was in covenant, in league, with me to fulfill His promise of recompense. This is true for anyone who has been unjustly dealt a violent and blatant blow. God hates thievery and crime, and especially the spilling of innocent blood. He will repay.

Notice what is meant by God being "in league" with us to bring about repayment for what the thief has stolen. Being "in league" implies working together for a common goal; it implies mutual assistance. It implies that *we have a part* in this covenant with God where He will "give [us our] recompense."

ENCOURAGE OURSELVES IN THE LORD

The story of David and Ziklag is an excellent illustration of how God is "in league" with us:

And it came to pass, when David and his men were come to Ziklag on the third day, that the Amalekites had invaded the south, and Ziklag, and smitten Ziklag, and burned it with fire; and had taken the women captives, that were therein: they slew not any, either great or small, but carried them away, and went on their way.

So David and his men came to the city, and, behold, it was burned
with fire; and their wives, and their sons, and their daughters,
were taken captives. Then David and the people that were with
him lifted up their voice and wept, until they had no more power
to weep.

1 Samuel 30:1-4

I would call this an unwelcome, discouraging circumstance. It was a violent, blatant robbery where the enemy took what did not belong to him, the people closest to the hearts of these men of God—their families. David had been fighting for the Lord, only to come home and find his own household taken captive. For all he knew, they were dead. Can we imagine our town burned, our house nothing but a foundation, our belongings scattered, and not a loved one in sight?

We must realize that the enemy will attack us whether we are working faithfully for the Lord or not. He doesn't care if we are sinning or if our lives are on the road to godly maturity. He wants to hand us the worst day of our lives—all day, every day.

God did not say that we would not have bad days, but He did say that those bad days would not prosper against you. He did not say that no weapon that is formed against you shall be able to come against you. Instead, He said, "No weapon that is formed against you shall prosper" (Isaiah 54:17 NKJV).

That's what happened to David. The enemy's weapons came against him, but David made some wise choices, and God caused those weapons to fail. First of all, David "encouraged himself in the LORD his God" (1 Samuel 30:6). In the midst of his own grief and loss, David's people wanted to stone him. Remember, sometimes your enemies may point an accusing finger at you for having been responsible for their unjust assaults when you were not at fault. David did not let the thief win.

And David was greatly distressed; for the people spake of stoning him, because the soul of all the people was grieved, every man for his sons and for his daughters: but David encouraged himself in the LORD his God.

1 Samuel 30:6

David encouraged himself in the Lord (something we will discuss in the chapter, "Comfort and Beauty, Joy, and Praise"). I'd like to point out that David had been anointed by Samuel to become the next king of Israel in Saul's stead. (1 Samuel 16:12-13.) He had played his harp for Saul and caused an evil spirit to depart. (1 Samuel 16:23.) He had defied and killed the Philistine giant, Goliath. (1 Samuel 17:51.) He was taken to King Saul's palace and set "over the men of war, and… accepted in the sight of all the people" (1 Samuel 18:5)—only to have Saul throw his javelin at him and pursue him as his enemy. Jealousy and rage had possessed Saul. He was out to kill David.

In 1 Samuel 22:2, David is found in a cave—*a far cry from the palace.* He is found with four hundred distressed, indebted, and discontented men from Israel—the rebels and rejects of that society—*a far cry from being king over Israel.* Imagine sleeping shoulder to shoulder with men like these who were full of turmoil. The mood in that cave must have been incredibly discouraging, but David did not become like them. Rather than be infected, he became infectious. He had a fire inside him that those four hundred men caught. When they came out of the cave, they were a great fighting army and he was their captain. This is what happens when we encourage ourselves in the Lord instead of becoming overwhelmed by circumstances.

Pursue, Overtake, and Recover All

After David encouraged himself in the Lord, then he sought the Lord.

And David said to Abiathar the priest, Ahimelech's son, I pray thee, bring me hither the ephod. And Abiathar brought thither the ephod to David. And David enquired at the LORD, saying, Shall I pursue after this troop? shall I overtake them? And he answered him, Pursue: for thou shalt surely overtake them, and without fail recover all.

1 Samuel 30:7-8

I love the fact that David sought the Lord first and never tried to do things on his own.

David knew that God called people to be a part of a body. One of his psalms says, "God setteth the solitary in families" (Psalm 68:6). One of the enemy's main tactics is to isolate us and make us think we don't need others. David did not try to pretend that he had all the answers. He went to the proper man with the proper anointing and pursued an answer with him. It is so important that we stay connected to a church full of men and women who know how to pray to break every yoke of bondage. It is important that we go where people know their gifts in the kingdom and are not afraid to use them.

While David went to Abiathar to inquire of the Lord, Abiathar did not do David's praying for him. "And he [the Lord] answered him, Pursue: for thou shalt surely overtake them, and without fail recover all" (1 Samuel 30:8). God told David to pursue, overtake, and recover all.

THE BIG WHY

I believe the Lord is telling some of you reading this book: *Now is the time to inquire of Me. Now is the time to go after what the devil has taken from you—the years lost to discouragement, dissatisfaction, unforgiveness, or whatever it is you're dealing with. Now is the time to actively engage the enemies of your family, your life, and your calling.*

I'm sure that God is wanting hurting people to make a quality decision to stop weeping and to step out of anger and bitterness. Too many people are confused about who God is and what His plan is for their lives. He wants them to begin overtaking and recovering what they have lost. This is how God will recompense what the enemy has wrongfully done.

There is another lesson to be learned from David's story about God's plan for recompense. As David pursued the Amalekites, the band of robbers who terrorized the region, he came upon an Egyptian who had lost his strength and was lying in a field. David, the man who had encouraged himself just moments ago, became the encourager for *someone else*—this young man.

> *And they gave him a piece of a cake of figs, and two clusters of raisins: and when he had eaten, his spirit came again to him: for he had eaten no bread, nor drunk any water, three days and three nights.*
>
> *1 Samuel 30:12*

In your process to recover all that has been lost, you can become an encouragement to others. We see this happening with David. David was prophesied to be king over Israel, yet he had lost his family and was now living as an outcast in the land of the Philistines. Instead of passing right by the Egyptian in need, David took a moment to encourage him. Little did he know that by acting correctly and making the right choices, his whole life would change within seventy-two hours. At the end of three days' time, he would become king of Israel, get his family back, and receive forty years of plunder back from the Amalekites. Talk about recompense! Talk about going from our worst day to our best day! When you feel like giving up, you are usually close to breaking through.

We can pave the way for God to recompense, to repay what the enemy has wrongly taken, *by making right choices.* Remember that God gave us freedom of choice, and that means leverage—power or ability to act or to influence people, events, decisions, or even God. He has given us the power and ability to sway the course and outcome of things. We must encourage ourselves in the Lord. We must not allow ourselves to be isolated, but allow others to stand with us in prayer. We must inquire of the Lord, and then we must overtake and recover all. Attacks don't kill dreams. Only lack of pursuit can kill your dream!

Remember, God has put His treasure—His Spirit, His very power— in these earthen vessels of ours. (2 Corinthians 4:7.) We are "crucified with Christ: nevertheless [we] live; yet not [we], but Christ liveth in [us]" (Galatians 2:20). Jesus lives in us. He works through us to bring about His recompense. "Now unto him that is able to do exceeding abundantly above all that we ask or think, according to the power that worketh in us" (Ephesians 3:20). God is able to "do exceeding abundantly...according to the power [His power] that worketh in us" (emphasis mine). *We* must overtake and recover all. Overcoming attacks teaches us how not to fail!

David saw the Amalekites "spread abroad upon all the earth, eating and drinking, and dancing, because of all the great spoil that they had taken out of the land of the Philistines, and out of the land of Judah" (1 Samuel 30:16). Imagine how it would feel to come over the crest of a hill and see our enemies dancing as our wives and children sat captive in their camp. Imagine our enemies eating food prepared from our crops and livestock, drinking wine and reveling in the money they stole from our houses.

If we are anything like David, we would become righteously angry—which is what it sometimes takes to pursue, overtake, and recover all—and move into our God-given destiny. We can become righteously angry at what the enemy stole and how he is abusing our inheritance. We can set our jaws firm and refuse to go back to our burned-out old life. We can determine to recover all that we lost. Almost all victory happens when you've come to the edge of defeat. You can't lose by getting knocked down; you lose if you stay down.

> *And David recovered all that the Amalekites had carried away: and David rescued his two wives. And there was nothing lacking to them, neither small nor great, neither sons nor daughters, neither spoil, nor any thing that they had taken to them: David recovered all.*
>
> *1 Samuel 30:18-19*

Victory happens when you risk defeat.

IF THE THIEF BE FOUND...

Proverbs 6:30-31 is another example of how God feels about recompense: "Men do not despise a thief, if he steal to satisfy his soul when he is hungry; but if he be found, he shall restore sevenfold; he shall give all the substance of his house." There is a very important message in this verse. We must recognize who the *real* thief is so that we can find him and demand restoration.

The devil wants us to be going down rabbit trails forever, blaming the wrong person or entity for the tragedies of life. For example, if we think that people die because it is God's time for them to go—that nothing can happen without God's permission—then we will ignore the real culprit and never demand our just recompense. That's why it is so important that we understand the sovereignty of God. Way too often God gets blamed for the work of the devil. As long as we sit back mistakenly thinking that God can do absolutely *anything* and that He is in control of *everything*, we will remain confused about what is truly going on. We will assume that God has His hand in matters that He doesn't. Even worse, we will be questioning deep down on the inside, wondering just how much He truly loves us since He did not step in and do something about our situation.

We must understand that the devil's ultimate weapon is to convince us that the heart of God is turned against us—that *God* is the real enemy. That is what the serpent told Eve in the Garden of Eden. He convinced Eve that God was her problem, not her purpose. It is almost more than the child of God can bear to think, that God is not for us because He didn't come through for us when we needed Him, or so we think. Even more painful is thinking that God is working against us. Job fought those thoughts:

> *Is it good unto thee that thou shouldest oppress, that thou shouldest despise the work of thine hands, and shine upon the counsel of the wicked?*
>
> *Job 10:3*

*If I be wicked, woe unto me; and if I be righteous, yet will I not
lift up my head. I am full of confusion; therefore see thou mine
affliction; for it increaseth. Thou huntest me as a fierce lion: and
again thou shewest thyself marvellous upon me. Thou renewest
thy witnesses against me, and increaseth thine indignation upon
me; changes and war are against me. Wherefore then hast thou
brought me forth out of the womb? Oh that I had given up the
ghost, and no eye had seen me!*

Job 10:15-18

From all appearances, Job felt justified in assuming that God
was oppressing him, even despising and rejecting him, and favoring
the schemes of the wicked. Job asked God why He was opposing or
striving against him: "I will say unto God, Do not condemn me; shew
me wherefore thou contendest with me" (Job 10:2.) Job further pleads
his case:

*Oh that I knew where I might find him! that I might come
even to his seat!...Behold, I go forward, but he is not there; and
backward, but I cannot perceive him: on the left hand, where
he doth work, but I cannot behold him: he hideth himself on the
right hand, that I cannot see him.*

Job 23:3,8-9

Negative things can come against you in life, especially when you risk
moving ahead into God's will for you.

Job continued to pursue God for his life, even in his pain. This
proved to Job and his "friends" that he was never defeated. Job was
recompensed for his trouble. The captivity of Job was turned around.

He found the thief...and it wasn't God. Job confessed, "Therefore [I now see] I have [rashly] uttered what I did not understand, things too wonderful for me, which I did not know" (Job 42:3 AMP).

If you won't give up, the thief will be found out before you go to be with Christ. True champions in life are those hurting, confused people who even now are charging the gates of hell, and the gates of hell "shall not prevail against it" (Matthew 16:18). You are reading this book because you intend to get a taste—a big dose—here and now of the *restoration and recompense* that God has in store for eternity. To swim across a large river, you begin with just one stroke and one kick, and then you just keep kicking and stroking. That's why some people swim and others sink, even with the same set of circumstances. Keep kicking!

PART THREE

THE
SECOND
VISITATION

FOUR REASONS

After Jesus' first visitation, I returned to sleep almost immediately. The Lord woke me a second time at 4:22 A.M. Again Jesus got straight to the point and began talking to me. This time He spoke about why bad things happen to good people on the rare occasions when it seems faith has failed. He revealed four main reasons for this right out of Luke, chapter 13: cults and bad governments, the curse, lack of diligence, and evil spirits. With these four reasons, I believe we can explain the cause for almost every evil that takes place.

Chapter 6

BECAUSE OF CULTS
AND BAD GOVERNMENTS

The Lord referred me to Luke 13:1-2, which says, "There were present at that season some that told him of the Galilaeans, whose blood Pilate had mingled with their sacrifices. And Jesus answering said unto them, Suppose ye that these Galilaeans were sinners above all the Galilaeans, because they suffered such things?" Jesus was telling me that these Galileans were no different than anyone else, but it was bad government that sacrificed them and spread their blood on the cult's sacrifice. This was martyrdom.

Jesus gave me cults and bad governments as the first reason why bad things happen to good people. He said these are two entities that create martyrs. Even today, the Church is widely persecuted around the world. There are underground churches today just as there were during times of persecution in the early Church.

PERSECUTION OF THE EARLY CHURCH

Satan, from the time of the Church's inception, has wanted to defeat it in whatever way he can. He, "the thief," has come "to steal, and to kill, and to destroy" (John 10:10). He has worked through cults and bad governments, both individually and together, to accomplish his goal.

When the church at Smyrna, discussed in Revelation 2:8-11, was exposed to fierce persecution, the blood of the martyrs flowed:

And unto the angel of the church in Smyrna write; These things saith the first and the last, which was dead, and is alive; I know thy works, and tribulation, and poverty, (but thou art rich) and I know the blasphemy of them which say they are Jews, and are not, but are the synagogue of Satan. Fear none of those things which thou shalt suffer: behold, the devil shall cast some of you into prison, that ye may be tried; and ye shall have tribulation ten days: be thou faithful unto death, and I will give thee a crown of life. He that hath an ear, let him hear what the Spirit saith unto the churches; He that overcometh shall not be hurt of the second death.

The church's foes turned out to be religious people who were actually representatives of Satan. There was a Judaizing movement in the early Church that mixed the law with grace—that substituted works for grace. We will recognize this as the work of a cult.

In the letter to this church, Jesus indicated that more persecution was to come. The letters to the seven churches have symbolic as well as literal application. The tribulation of the Smyrna church that was to extend over ten days turned out to be ten periods of intense persecution at the hands of Roman emperors from A.D. 100-300. Here we have both the cult and bad government causing bad things to happen to people. During this period of time, the church experienced loss of property, poverty, times of meeting in caves and catacombs, and being hunted, arrested, tortured, burned alive, and fed to hungry lions.

CORRUPTION FROM WITHIN

The initial persecution of the church at Smyrna only resulted in God's body of believers growing in both size and quality. The blood of the martyrs became seed into the earth to propagate the church. In response, Satan tried a new tactic: the government and the world merged with the church at Pergamos, corrupted it from within, and created a church that was "wed" to the world and the government. Again bad government had its part. The Roman emperor Constantine, while stopping persecution and restoring seized property to Christians, paved the way for Satan to do even greater damage. His tactics changed from outright persecution to corrupting the church from within.

Again cults came into play. During Constantine's rule, a great controversy arose over the deity of Christ, giving rise to the cultish Arianism. Arius, a leader in the church in Alexandria, Egypt, was the main proponent of this false doctrine.

This has been just enough church history to support what the Lord was telling me out of Luke, chapter 13, about cults and bad government. Cults and bad government seem to be particularly damaging to God's people. It doesn't have to be obvious like Diocletian and his Roman government totally outlawing Christianity. They had public bonfires to burn all copies of Scriptures, prohibited all church meetings, burned all church buildings, burned Christians' homes, and tortured and martyred Christians—they tried to wipe Christianity entirely off the face of the earth. It can also be subtle like Constantine and his government, who appeared to be a friend and supporter of the church, while they quietly corrupted it and enticed it into an unholy alliance with the political system of the world.

CULTS DEFINED

But there were false prophets also among the people, even as there shall be false teachers among you, who privily shall bring in damnable heresies, even denying the Lord that bought them, and bring upon themselves swift destruction. And many shall follow their pernicious ways; by reason of whom the way of truth shall be evil spoken of.

2 Peter 2:1-2

The dictionary renders a *cult* as "a religion or sect considered to be false, unorthodox, or extremist, with members often living outside of conventional society under the direction of a charismatic leader." In much broader terms, a cult is a counterfeit religious group that comes in pretense of Christianity. While claiming to be Christian, these groups don't acknowledge Jesus Christ as their savior. Cults exist in the United States just as they exist around the world.

"Religion" or "religious" are key words in our discussion here. Because man is a spiritual being by nature, the easiest and most prevalent form of deception is religion. People will usually trust religious leaders who are supposedly the representatives of God. Therefore the Antichrist, the political leader during the Tribulation in the last days, uses the False Prophet to promote him. That's his diabolical partner in subduing the population of the earth. He doesn't use a famous movie star or sports figure or some exceptionally talented singer or a prominent, successful leader in business or industry or finance. He uses a "religious" man.

A plain and simple definition of religion is the service and worship of God or the supernatural. In the sense that this is directed toward the God of the Bible, there is a pure and undefiled religion that is good. But religion in a negative context—as in that which is ritual and not real—is what the Bible describes as "having a form of godliness, but denying the power thereof" (2 Timothy 3:5).

The Scripture that we quoted earlier speaks of "false teachers among you, who privily shall bring in damnable heresies, even denying the Lord that bought them" (2 Peter 2:1). What is surprising is that these false teachers rarely deny Jesus overtly; but they deny Him, nevertheless, in various subtle ways. Let me explain.

"RELIGIOUS" IS OKAY WITH THE DEVIL

While having numerous differences, one of the common characteristics of cults is that they teach that one can be saved by works. However, Ephesians 2:8 tells us, "For by grace are ye saved through faith; and that not of yourselves: it is the gift of God." If we can attain salvation through works, then the blood of Jesus was not necessary. To subscribe to salvation through works is to deny the necessity and power of the blood of Jesus which is the source of the Christian's power.

Forasmuch as ye know that ye were not redeemed with corruptible things, as silver and gold, from your vain conversation received by tradition from your fathers; but with the precious blood of Christ, as of a lamb without blemish and without spot.

1 Peter 1:18-19

In whom we have redemption through his blood, the forgiveness of sins, according to the riches of his grace.

Ephesians 1:7

And they overcame him by the blood of the Lamb, and by the word of their testimony; and they loved not their lives unto the death.

Revelation 12:11

To deny the power of the blood is to deny the deity of Jesus—that is antichrist. There you have it—"false teachers among you, who privily shall bring in damnable heresies, *even denying the Lord that bought them*" (v. 1, emphasis mine). "False teachers" and their cults deny the Lord by refuting that Jesus Christ came in the flesh. This cultish belief is called Gnosticism.

The Bible defines "religion" in its negative context as "having a form of godliness, but denying the power thereof" (2 Timothy 3:5). The real power behind godliness is the blood of Jesus, but religion wants us to think that it is works. Religion is man's way to get to God. It negates the power of Jesus' work at Calvary. Its primary thrust is to require something of us—works—before we can approach God or expect God to move for us. This leaves out the blood of Jesus which is the only thing that gives us access to God's presence.

We need to note that religion has works but faith has works, too. Religion's works are a regimen or ritual of do's and don'ts to make us think *we are earning our way to God.* Faith's works are actions that correspond to our belief in God, positive responses to what God has *already* done. Jesus closed the gap between us and God because of His redemptive work on the cross. This enables us to lay hold of our inheritance in Him. Faith's works are outward evidence that we truly believe in our hearts what Jesus has done for us. Religion keeps us always assessing our relationship with God based on what we do and do not do. It puts us on a treadmill going nowhere, because we never seem to measure up. Our good never seems to be good enough, and our bad is always too bad.

Satan doesn't mind our being "religious." The greatest deception today is that many Christians and many churches are controlled by a "religious" spirit. Satan's goal is to keep us from truly knowing and experiencing the love of God—the greatest force on the earth. Satan doesn't mind our being religious; he doesn't mind our believing in just enough Bible doctrine to make us think we're okay. He'd like to keep us sitting on the church pew living in pain and grief and saying, *Not my will, but Thy will be done.* He'd like to steal our victory.

It is part of man's nature to know that there is a God—even if that man claims to be an atheist. It is also part of man's nature to want to draw near to God in worship and in fellowship. These are inherent things. Paul explains it like this:

> *Because that which may be known of God is manifest in them; for God hath shewed it unto them. For the invisible things of him from the creation of the world are clearly seen, being understood by the things that are made, even his eternal power and Godhead; so that they are without excuse.*
>
> *Romans 1:19-20*

> *For that which is known about God is evident to them and made plain in their inner consciousness, because God [Himself] has shown it to them.*
>
> *Romans 1:19 AMP*

It's in us to know that there is a God and to want to worship Him, but Satan has determined to pervert this.

Satan wants to re-direct our worship of God. If he can't get us to openly and purposefully worship him, he wants us to worship idols. If he can't get us to worship idols, he wants us to settle for worshiping man (where Satan doesn't get direct worship but, at least, God doesn't either). If he can't get us to worship man, he wants us to settle for worshiping God, but leave Jesus out of the picture. The spirit of the world is okay with God, but not with Jesus Christ. If the devil can't get us to settle for worshiping God without Jesus, then he wants us to at least leave out the Holy Spirit. If not, then at least leave out the Holy Spirit's power and manifestations. He'll take anything less than the best. Our best is worshiping God as individuals who have a relationship with Him through Jesus Christ and who know Him in the power of His Holy Spirit with manifestations to boot.

CULTS AND BAD GOVERNMENTS TODAY

Are we understanding what cults are all about? More than ever, they are prolific and rampant:

> Since the 1960s, there has been a burgeoning...of independent entrepreneurial groups that go into the mind-manipulation and personality-change business. Myriads of false messiahs, quacks, and leaders of cults and thought-reform groups have emerged... They recruit the curious, the unaffiliated, the trusting, and the altruistic. They promise intellectual, spiritual, political, social, and self-actualization utopias. These modern-day pied pipers offer, among other things, pathways to God, salvation, revolution, personal development, enlightenment, perfect health, psychological growth, egalitarianism, channels to speak with 35,000-year-old "entities," life in ecospheres, and contact with extraterrestrial beings.[1]

There are dangerous cults today that would be considered abusive and exploitative of their followers. Areas of abuse would include "finances, physical labor, child abuse and neglect, medical neglect, sexual exploitation and/or psychological and emotional abuse."[2] More contemporary cults that have exhibited over-the-top destructive behavior have been:

> *...the Waco Davidians, the cult suicides of "Heaven's Gate" and the Solar Temple of Switzerland and the suicide/murder of almost one thousand members of the Peoples Temple ordered by Jim Jones. In 1995 the Japanese cult known as Aum, the followers of Shoko Asahara, gassed the subways of Tokyo with the deadly poison gas, sarin, killing twelve and injuring thousands of citizens. Perhaps the most deaths ever caused by a single cult in modern history can be attributed to the "Movement for the Restoration of the Ten Commandments" of Uganda. Shortly after the turn of the century, 780 bodies were found after a reign of terror that included murder and possibly mass suicide. But due to the isolated circumstances of the group many believe all the bodies will never be recovered, placing the actual loss of life much higher, possibly greater than Jonestown.[3]*

Cults are used to cause bad things to happen to God's children by robbing us materially and physically, even leading to martyrdom. They are instruments of Satan to lead people astray into lies, deceit, confusion, and ultimately hell. People involved in cults end up like the seduced son in Proverbs, chapter 5, whom his father tried to warn:

> *Remove thy way far from her, and come not nigh the door of her house: Lest thou give thine honour unto others, and thy years unto the cruel: Lest strangers be filled with thy wealth; and thy labours be in the house of a stranger; and thou mourn at the last, when thy flesh and thy body are consumed.*

> *Proverbs 5:8-11*

THE BIG WHY

Bad governments, too, can be blamed for bad things happening to good people. Bad governments have been responsible for horrific, godless, political massacres such as Ugandan Idi Amin's murder of 300,000 of his countrymen. Pol Pot turned his country of Cambodia into a blood-bath as he slaughtered one million Cambodians. Both of these despots were in power in the 1970s.

There was the Algerian Civil War between the Algerian government and various Islamist rebel groups which began in 1991. It is estimated to have cost between 150,000 and 200,000 lives. Islamic extremism has all the same characteristics of a cult, and has done innumerable damage to innocent people, as experienced in Algeria:

> *Algeria was wracked by massacres of intense brutality and unprecedented size... Typically targeting entire villages or neighborhoods and disregarding the age and sex of victims, [terrorists] killed tens, and sometimes hundreds, of civilians at a time....the Rais and Bentalha massacres in particular shocked worldwide observers. Pregnant women were sliced open, children were hacked to pieces or dashed against walls, men's limbs were hacked off one by one, and, as the attackers retreated, they would kidnap young women to keep as sex slaves.*[4]

The attitude of the attackers was:

> *We have the whole night to rape your women and children, drink your blood. Even if you escape today, we'll come back tomorrow to finish you off! We're here to send you to your God!*[5]

The effect of cults and bad governments on Christians is undisputed.

CULTS AND BAD GOVERNMENTS

The threat of bad governments has not been merely in regard to material and physical robbery of people, even martyrdom. Bad governments seduce the Church to compromise its stand for God—to settle for moral degradation in legislation, public behavior, the arts, education, the media, and so on. They want the Church to go by the world's way of doing things instead of God's. Today, some so-called Christian groups even endorse abortion, the innocent slaughter of millions of babies every year worldwide. This is all due to bad government policies that have said it's a "choice." It's not a choice, it's a *soul*.

We have bad governments and we have cults in our midst today, with the most effective cults arising within what is acknowledged as Christianity. They water salvation down to a doctrine of works. They leave out Scriptures. They misinterpret and twist the Scriptures. They add to the Scriptures. They hide behind Scriptures. They hide behind the name "Christianity." They overall are "ravening wolves" in "sheep's clothing" (Matthew 7:15). Something *ravening* is something that seeks to "plunder or prey, to feed or devour voraciously." Cults are wicked, even eternally deadly. Either separately or working together with bad government, these have been instruments in Satan's hands for inflicting pain and death on God's children throughout the ages.

Chapter 7

BECAUSE OF THE CURSE

The second reason for why bad things happen to good people is found in Luke 13:4 NKJV, which says, "Or those eighteen on whom the tower in Siloam fell and killed them, do you think that they were worse sinners than all other men who dwelt in Jerusalem?" The Lord told me, "The second reason that bad things can happen to good people is because of the curse. Take these eighteen men—they were standing in the wrong place at the wrong time by chance or by accident." *By chance or by accident*—that's the expression that the Lord used.

The Lord said that because of Adam's sin, the curse is now in operation in the earth. Because of the curse, accidents can happen. These eighteen men were at Siloam near the pool of Siloam mentioned in John 9, where the blind man washed his eyes after Jesus anointed them with clay. (John 9:6,7.) Apparently there was a large tower there, and all of these men were standing in the wrong place at the wrong time. There were probably more than eighteen men there, because they would have been standing around that pool, and that pool could have had over 150 people around it. There would have been a sizeable number of people gathered around that pool on a regular basis. When the tower fell, eighteen men were killed, and it was an accident, pure and simple. Accidents can happen because of the curse that is in the earth today. However, unlike the eighteen men killed in Siloam, we have the promise of eternal life: "Or those eighteen on whom the tower in

Siloam fell and killed them, do you think that they were worse sinners than all other men who dwelt in Jerusalem? I tell you, no; but unless you repent you will all likewise perish" (Luke 13:4,5 NKJV).

WHAT IS THE CURSE?

In the Garden of Eden, man fell into sin and death. His disobedience led to punishment—to a curse. Hatred, violence, selfishness and strife—all products of sin—came with this curse. The first son born into this newly-cursed world was a murderer: Cain, who killed his brother Abel.

Even the ground was cursed:

Cursed is the ground for thy sake; in sorrow shalt thou eat of it all the days of thy life; thorns also and thistles shall it bring forth to thee; and thou shalt eat the herb of the field; in the sweat of thy face shalt thou eat bread, till thou return unto the ground.

Genesis 3:17-19

But on the cross of Calvary, Jesus took on our sin and death *and* the curse:

Christ hath redeemed us from the curse of the law, being made a curse for us: for it is written, Cursed is every one that hangeth on a tree: that the blessing of Abraham might come on the Gentiles through Jesus Christ; that we might receive the promise of the Spirit through faith.... Wherefore the law was our schoolmaster to bring us unto Christ, that we might be justified by faith. But after that faith is come, we are no longer under a schoolmaster.

Galatians 3:13-14, 24-25

Jesus wore a crown of thorns and this is significant ("cursed is the ground...thorns also and thistles shall it bring forth"). The curse was placed on Him. He took the place of not only one murderer—Barabbas—but He took on the sins of the world, and that included *every* murderer. "For he hath made him to be sin for us, who knew no sin" (2 Corinthians 5:21). He, who knew no sin, became sin for us. On the cross, Jesus became every wicked person, every evil thought, word, and deed deserving of death and hell. We brought on the curse, but Jesus took it upon Himself and got rid of it for us. He didn't just take the curse upon Himself; He became the curse for us, just as He became sin for us.

From the cross, Jesus said, "It is finished" (John 19:30). Everything God the Father had planned for our salvation has been fulfilled. Our sins are covered and there is no more price to pay. God's judgment against us has been satisfied. "There is therefore now no condemnation to them which are in Christ Jesus" (Romans 8:1). We don't have to to guess where we are with God based on our works, and wonder if our good works outweigh the bad.

Now, if we brought on the curse, and Jesus took it upon Himself and got rid of it for us, then how can I say that accidents can happen because of the curse that is in the earth today? Jesus got rid of the curse, but we still live in a world where the curse is in effect. We've been redeemed from the curse, but not removed from it. Because of the curse of sin, pain, problems, death, accidents, and other bad experiences that Adam and Eve loosed upon mankind, we are potentially subject to the same set of circumstances that our forefathers were. There will come a day when Jesus will remove and redeem the earth from all of the curse, but until that time, we are still living in an imperfect place called planet earth. This is where accidents do happen every day. Things just don't always go right.

Jesus didn't just come to deal with our sin problem. He came to give us life, and abundant life at that. (John 10:10.) He came to deal with the curse as well, which will stand in the way of our experiencing abundant life. Some people who are saved are not aware that they are redeemed from the curse, and so they don't grab hold of the abundant life that Jesus has provided for them through faith in His redemptive work.

As I pointed out in a previous discussion, we are exposed to and affected by the sins, foolishness, and ignorance of others and the resulting consequences. To a degree, we can be affected by others who are still living under the curse. For example, let's say that someone was not diligent while building the tower of Siloam. This foolishness could have resulted in the accident that occurred that day and took the lives of eighteen men. In the next chapter we will see how *lack of diligence* is connected to the curse.

WORD CURSES

Most of the world is still living under the curse. The earth itself is still experiencing this. No doubt that is what Paul describes in Romans 8:22, which says, "For we know that the whole creation groaneth and travaileth in pain together until now." The verse preceding this says, "Because the creature itself also shall be delivered from the bondage of corruption into the glorious liberty of the children of God" (v. 21). The earth itself is still experiencing the curse because of the people who have not yet come into the glory of God.

A *curse*, in everyday language, is an evil that has been invoked upon a person or group. Unknowingly, we as Christians can walk around having evil invoked upon us, even by ourselves. One of the main ways that we do this is through the power of our tongue. "Death and life are in the power of the tongue: and they that love it shall eat the fruit thereof" (Proverbs 18:21). Death is part of the curse. We must choose not to live under this curse.

Just as faith obtains our salvation, faith obtains life instead of death. The words that come out of our mouth demonstrate our belief that Jesus has come to give us life because "out of the abundance of the heart the mouth speaketh" (Matthew 12:34). If we speak words of death, we don't truly believe that Jesus has provided life instead of death. It's not a matter of us through "right" confession demanding anything of Jesus. It is not a matter of us "working" to get something from Jesus through proper confession. It is a matter of us appropriating the life that He has provided by believing that He has already done this for us. Our confession is the agreement of our heart being voiced out loud. It is evidence of our faith. The exercising of our faith allows for the release of life, the God kind of life. We overcome "by the blood of the Lamb, and by the word of [our] testimony" (Revelation 12:11). Our testimony appropriates what Jesus accomplished by the blood.

At the time that God said, "Let us make man in our image" (Genesis 1:26), what was He doing? He was creating...*by the power of His words*, He was creating. "And God *said*, Let there be light.... And God *said*, Let there be a firmament.... And God *said*, Let the waters under the heaven be gathered together.... And God *said*, Let the earth bring forth grass.... And God *said*, Let there be lights in the firmament..." (Genesis 1:3,6,9,11,14). Having been created in God's image, we have been created to create by the power of our words. We bring what God has already provided in the spiritual realm into manifestation in the natural realm. If we do not understand this, we can be saved and still operate as if we are living under the curse.

> *A man shall eat good by the fruit of his mouth: but the soul of the transgressors shall eat violence. He that keepeth his mouth keepeth his life: but he that openeth wide his lips shall have destruction.*
>
> *Proverbs 13:2-3*

Because of the curse, bad things can happen to people, even good people. We can speak negative things and curse ourselves, reaping death in various ways—we can "eat violence." We can also fail to speak to our mountains, and they will not be removed. Because of the curse, good things that *should* happen *don't* happen, and that, too, is a bad thing. Not only can we fail by speaking negative things, many good things may never happen if we fail to speak good things. We should endeavor to create "life," abundant life in our personal world.

THE CURSE OF THE LAW

I've already shared how Satan is okay with "religion" or our being "religious." He knows that man is a spiritual being and that the easiest and most prevalent form of deception is religion. So if he can get "religion" or "religious" attached to something that falls short of true Christianity, he can get us sidetracked and settling for less in God. That's bad, and can result in bad things in our lives rather than the goodness of God.

Religion will act as if its aim is to have power with God. Religion will give the appearance of "godliness," only to have "a form of godliness, but denying the power thereof" (2 Timothy 3:5). Religion robs us of power with God more quickly than just about anything. How does it do this? It wants us to live by what we can accomplish in our own ability—prayer, fasting, reading the Word, holy living—rather than putting our trust in the blood of Jesus. While all of these activities are definitely things we want to have going on in our lives, they should not take the place of what was accomplished by Jesus' blood. We do these things because Jesus saved us and because Jesus made us righteous—not to get Him to save us or for us to become righteous.

Knowing that a man is not justified by the works of the law, but by the faith of Jesus Christ, even we have believed in Jesus Christ, that we might be justified by the faith of Christ, and not by the works of the law: for by the works of the law shall no flesh be justified.

Galatians 2:16

There is an important message here for the born-again believer who has let the enemy divert his eyes from the Cross to works—to reaching perfection or acceptance by God through his own efforts. Righteousness is only available through belief in Jesus Christ.

We are not talking about doing away with the law and becoming a lawless generation. Jesus did not come to do away with the law but to fulfill it. It was through the law that Paul received a consciousness of sin, but the law gave him no power to overcome it. Therefore, he turned from the law as the means of acceptance with God. (Galatians 2:19.) Through Jesus' death on the cross, Christ did for us what we could not do for ourselves. His work, not ours, removes the curse upon us because of our disobedience to the law. (Galatians 3:13.) By faith in the finished work at Calvary—not our works—we receive the benefits provided by Jesus' death, which include life and the power to live that life.

We must *not* put the works of the law in the place of grace and faith in the blood atonement. Legalism will snuff God and the abundant life He has for us right out of our lives. Legalism will rob us of good things coming our way and will set us up for ashes instead of beauty, mourning instead of the oil of joy, and heaviness instead of the garment of praise—curses that Jesus was anointed to break over our lives.

INIQUITY'S CURSE

Multitudes, Christians included, are living under the curse of iniquity because they do not understand what iniquity is. Iniquity oftentimes doesn't exist in an individual's life because he chose to have it. It is inherited. It is weakness in a person's nature for a particular sin that's inherited from his forefathers. It holds families in bondage for generations. Iniquity is formed in someone by continued, repetitive sins and overriding the conviction of the Holy Spirit against a sin. Even a dedicated, veteran Christian may find the bondage of iniquity a persistent problem He may, in trying to deal with it, be caught up in a sin-repentance cycle that leads him nowhere, feeling more defeated than ever. As such, iniquity's damage strongly reflects the curse.

Because iniquity is such a misunderstood subject, it has been dealt with ineffectively and has been allowed to do major damage to the body of Christ. For that reason, I want to deal with this subject. This is a good place to do it since we're talking about the curse as a main reason for why bad things happen to good people.

GENERATIONAL CURSES?

Today the body of Christ has a lot of teaching on the subject of generational curses, which is not necessarily a scriptural term. The thought is right, but the terminology is not. I believe the term God uses to describe what some call "generational curses" is *iniquity*. That's why the children of Israel repeatedly fell into the same kinds of sins. (Exodus 34:7.) Iniquity is why some people get hooked up to God, only to fall into the same sin trap that plagued their lives before salvation. This same sin trap habitually ensnared their ancestors.

There is a difference between one-time mistakes and a repetitive pattern of sin ingrained in us. Perhaps we've observed someone whose sin problem kept him from maturing in God. Or maybe we have known the desperation of a vice that seemed impossible to defeat. Many Christians who sincerely love Jesus Christ are constantly tripped up by repetitive sin. These individuals seem to have placed everything about their lives under the blood of Christ except one or two areas that seem constantly to cause them trouble. These one or two things keep cropping up throughout their lives, creating havoc and keeping them from living in the total victory promised to Christians in the Word of God. Every time these individuals appear to be getting ahead in the things of God, these particular problem areas surface again, rearing their ugly heads, so to speak—and all spiritual progress is suddenly lost. Those old sin problems seem to reach right out, grab them, and drag them down.

The Bible repeatedly mentions iniquity, and yet iniquity is an area in which many modern-day Christians lack spiritual insight and understanding. Isaiah 53:5 says that Jesus was *"wounded for our transgressions."* Transgressions—that refers to sin. It also says that He *"was bruised for our iniquities."* Iniquities—here we have those inherent weaknesses, or propensities, in the soul or mind toward sin that keep tripping up some Christians. The good news is that the work of Jesus upon the cross at Calvary has already purchased freedom from sin and victory over iniquity.

IT'S A GENE...ISN'T IT?

Every physical thing about us is inherited. The same human genes are reproduced repeatedly, over and over again from one generation to the next, perfectly passing down traits ranging from hair and eye color to height. Not just physical traits are inherited. Things like talents, abilities—even musical gifts—personality quirks, and small things like handwriting are also passed down. While some inherited traits are easy to spot, other things are less readily apparent.

Our weaknesses are also inherited. The Bible calls them iniquity, formed through repetitive sin, producing a weakness or propensity for certain sins. Whether they are character traits present in a person's nature, ungodly attitudes, or tendencies toward certain sins, these weaknesses are passed down from one generation to the next. They will continue to be passed down until we or someone in our family repents before God and puts these iniquities under the blood of Jesus. The Bible says that when a person repents, he will bear the brunt of iniquity no longer. (Ezekiel 18.)

We can be delivered from inherited iniquity. We can walk out from under undesirable, ungodly ancestral traits that made us like our ancestors. When we understand what iniquity is, we will recognize it instantly when it rears its ugly head. Then we will be able to break its power over us. By faith we can speak to iniquity and apply the finished work of Calvary to break its power over our lives.

ADDICTIVE THOUGHTS

Echoes from the past and sinful behaviors lead to addictive thought patterns. We become addicted to a way of thinking. I believe every person is an "addict" in some way, for better or for worse. Some people can look at a billboard, and it will set off a chain reaction of visual pictures in their imaginations that can take weeks and months to stop. That's why the world sells sex. Not even chewing gum is advertised without showing a provocative body. The world knows that people are mentally addicted to different thoughts.

Many people are addicted to thought patterns based on past experience. These thought patterns are as addictive as a drug. Because of past experience, some people automatically mistrust when they should trust, doubt when they should believe, and react negatively when truth is in front of them. They are addicted to thought patterns that produce an automatic behavior.

INIQUITIES, NOT DEMONS

It's sad that some people have gone to all sorts of preachers to get victory over repetitive sin. Some people believe they have a demon every time they sin, and they think they have to go get it cast out. It's one of the saddest errors in present teaching in the body of Christ—that people who are saved and filled with the Holy Spirit can also be demon-possessed. Such people simply were never delivered from iniquity. Iniquity has caused so many people to be tripped up with repeat sin. Parents who drink will often raise children who drink. Parents who abuse their children will often raise children who become abusive parents. Children who were molested often grow up to become child molesters themselves. Some psychologists today blame this on environmental living or association. They say it's all in how a person is raised. Though that may produce the same end result, the Bible calls it iniquity.

SUPPRESSING INIQUITY IS NOT ENOUGH

Some people continually suppress iniquity, but denying the existence of iniquity is not the same as receiving deliverance from it. If they suppress iniquity, it may still crop up later even more powerfully than if they had stopped along the way to deal with it. That's why some people who used to drink find themselves returning to alcohol after many years of sobriety. If they did not receive deliverance from their iniquity, the devil may still attempt to turn them toward alcohol. Whatever the weakness, the devil will try to find it and apply pressure. He will keep them in guilt or condemnation because of their mental attraction to their iniquity, even if they are strong enough to keep from acting out their sin.

"Oh, no—I'm a Christian," we say. Yes, even some Christians have to fight to keep from telling lies. Other Christians have a weakness for pornography. They may say, "Oh, I don't want to do that"; but they are powerless against its lure. Eventually they are drawn back into its snare. Because they do not understand how to overcome iniquity, they try to suppress it. If that's not effective, then they feel it's a hopeless cause and they simply roll over and give in to it.

HOW GOD DEALT WITH
MY OWN INIQUITIES

Even my Hallam hot temper was an iniquity. It's the thing God needed me to fix before I could become a preacher. I ran from the ministry for over twenty-five years because I had a hot temper. I ran when I could have been preaching the gospel and accomplishing God's purpose for my life. When I was growing up, preachers would come through town, and prophesy that God had called me to preach. But I didn't want to preach, and I ran.

God never let up. He kept saying, *You're not doing what I told you to do.* Sometimes I'd get bold and talk back and say, "What I'm doing must be the will of God for my life because things are going so well." I had decided I'd be a multimillionaire and a deacon—in that order. I had pride in my iniquity. Many people are never delivered from their iniquities because they have become prideful about their sin. They gave up the battle because of so many past defeats.

When I was in business, I didn't want anything to do with full-time ministry, but God kept bringing it up. Finally I couldn't run anymore. I said, "Okay, God, if preaching is what You want me to do, I'm ready to serve You. I'll preach the gospel. I'll teach the Word. I don't care what You want me to do—I'll do it. Just open the doors." Even as I prayed, I knew I had certain character traits that would have to go—like my hot temper. It had caused me trouble all of my life. It caused me trouble in high school, in college, in the service, on the job, at the mechanic, and on the highway. It even caused me trouble in church when it was time to deal with other Christians. How in the world could I preach with a temper like mine? I said, "God, I need your help with this thing."

That's when God began to reveal to me the truth about iniquity. He said, *You have iniquity in your life, and you have not dealt with it through the blood of Jesus.* He showed me what it was and what to do about it.

Once the power of iniquity was broken in my life, it was easy to line up with God's will and start preaching. I said, "All I have is one life. I can't wait until after I become a multimillionaire to serve God. If I'm going to serve God, I'd better do it now."

I was at a conference in 1980 when God revealed to me what iniquity was and how to be set free from it forever. When I got home, I went to the bedroom, knelt down beside the bed, and said, "God, if You're real, then I know You can deal with every sin in my life." I began to talk to Him personally, and that's when He began to give me insight about iniquity.

Get Honest with God

Sometimes we have to get honest with God. Sometimes everybody else is not the problem—we are the problem. God showed me that I was the problem; iniquity had been passed down to me. He showed me that Jesus had already been bruised for my iniquity. As I saw the truth, I cried out, "Jesus, I believe You were bruised for my iniquity. I confess this weakness—jealousy—in my life, and I ask that Your power flow into that area to bring deliverance." As I've said before: Our life of faith is a response to God's power, not our own works.

As I spoke, fear departed and faith rose up in me. I said repeatedly, day after day, that I was no longer a man with a hot temper. Why? Because Jesus was bruised for those iniquities. Those iniquities had been controlling me and limiting my horizons for many years. When

God helped me understand the nature of iniquity, I was able to apply His Word, by faith, to overcome my spiritual stumbling blocks.

Do you know what happened next? Victory. When faith comes, so does victory. Not long after I started pastoring, God said to me, *If you'll obey My Word, no one will be able to keep you from doing what I have told you to do.* I became a happy preacher that very minute, because I believed God when He spoke. I became perfectly at peace with pastoring—the very thing I ran from for so long. I was happy because God had revealed how to conquer the areas of iniquity in my life that had been causing me to stumble—causing me to run. I found that I could obey His voice and fulfill the call on my life.

This is a message every preacher needs to take to heart. Many preachers who have fallen into scandal did so due to their own iniquities. It was not because they did not love God. It was because they had weaknesses in their personalities, their minds, their wills, or their emotions that had not been put under the blood of Jesus. The iniquities that were passed down to them from their forefathers eventually caused their downfall.

THE DIFFERENCE BETWEEN SIN AND INIQUITY

First John 2, describes *transgression* as the willful breaking of God's law, or the *external* manifestation of sin. A transgression is something that can be seen on the outside. It is sin made manifest. What does the Bible say about sin made manifest? It says that Jesus was wounded for it. "He was wounded for our transgressions" (Isaiah 53:5). Calvary took care of sin for you and me. Jesus' death on the cross purchased our forgiveness for sins and gave us the power to stand before God, sanctified.

Isaiah 53:5 also says, "He was bruised for our iniquities." A bruise is not always outwardly visible. The worst bruises are internal. Jesus was "bruised for our iniquities"—the things that are hidden beneath the surface, inherent weaknesses that cause us to sin when they are acted upon. Calvary covered both our *transgressions* and our *iniquities.* Jesus died for the sins that are outwardly visible, as well as latent, inherent internal tendencies toward sin that the devil uses to really put pressure on us.

Let's look at Isaiah 53:5 in its entirety: "But he was wounded for our transgressions, he was bruised for our iniquities: the chastisement of our peace was upon him; and with his stripes we are healed." Jesus paid the price once and for all for all our iniquities. There was no other way for mankind to be released from iniquity. Ephesians 2:3 states: "Among whom also we all had our conversation in times past in the lusts of our flesh, fulfilling the desires of the flesh and of the mind; and were by nature the children of wrath, even as others." What does that passage of Scripture say? It says we were by nature the children of wrath. Before what? Before Calvary.

Before we were born again and filled with the Holy Spirit, that nature ruled our lives. That nature still remains in some people even after they are born again. Even though they are born again, these individuals do not live consistent, godly lives because they still have iniquities. Romans 5:12 says that because one man sinned, death passed on to all mankind. Because we all inherited the iniquitous nature, a person could conceivably live a perfect life, never commit one sin, and still not be found perfect before God until he receives Jesus Christ as Savior.

The iniquitous nature, present on the inside even when dormant, carries the tendency to sin even if no sin has actually been committed.

That's why none of us can save ourselves. Every one of us needs Jesus. He is the only one who can deal with both sin and the sin nature. Thank God for grace!

WHAT HAPPENED AT CALVARY

At Calvary, Christ addressed all three dimensions of our being— spirit, soul, and body. He took care of the spiritual realm by offering eternal life in the presence of His Father. He took care of the external, physical realm when He died for our sins. He was wounded for our transgressions. (Isaiah 53:5.) Just as a *wound* is external, a transgression is an outward, external breaking of God's commands. Jesus was wounded externally for our transgressions. He also took care of our inner man—our soul: our mind, will, and our emotions. He was bruised for our iniquities. A *bruise* is internal bleeding that cannot be seen on the outside. All our iniquitous urges to sin can be brought under the blood of Christ so that our souls also experience full deliverance as promised in the Word of God.

Isaiah 53:5 also tells us that Jesus was chastised for our peace. If we have iniquity within us, constantly keeping us in turmoil, we don't have peace. There are many people who are saved and filled with the Holy Spirit, yet they have no peace. They walk around in failure their whole lives because they are bound by iniquity. Jesus purchased our peace on the cross at Calvary. God wants more than for us to be redeemed spiritually. He wants more than just a covenant with our flesh. He wants all of us—spirit, flesh, mind, will, and emotions—and the finished work of Christ on the cross purchased that for us. He will give us His power to subdue the iniquities that have caused us so much trouble. He will cast our sin into the sea and subdue our iniquities. We can break the curse! That's powerful!

THE BIG WHY

Far too often we claim the legal experiences that belong to us in Christ Jesus, but never experience the manifestations of what legally has been purchased for us by our Lord. The Bible says that Christ redeemed us from the curse of the law. (Galatians 3:13.) I contend that one drop of Jesus' blood would have redeemed all of humanity. The only divine thing on this planet when Jesus walked with us was the blood inside His body. Everything else was carnal. One drop of His blood could have totally anesthetized all the problems that Adam loosed on earth. The shedding of blood removed the wages of sin and the effects of sin. Christ redeemed us from *all* the curses of hell. I get pretty excited when I think about that.

Humanity was taken into captivity through the sin of Adam and Eve. We had nothing to do with it. Death entered the blood—spiritual death became our inheritance, and it brought physical death, as well. We didn't earn the curse. We did not willfully sin to choose the curse. We didn't deserve it, yet Christ paid the price for my freedom—and for yours. He bought us like a slave on an auction block, and then set us free. He has released us to live free of iniquity...free of the curse.

Chapter 8

BECAUSE OF
LACK OF DILIGENCE

Jesus continued to speak to me, referring to verses 6 through 9 of Luke 13 that had to do with the parable of the barren fig tree.

He spake also this parable; A certain man had a fig tree planted in his vineyard; and he came and sought fruit thereon, and found none. Then said he unto the dresser of his vineyard, Behold, these three years I come seeking fruit on this fig tree, and find none: cut it down; why cumbereth it the ground? And he answering said unto him, Lord, let it alone this year also, till I shall dig about it, and dung it: And if it bear fruit, well: and if not, then after that thou shalt cut it down.

Apparently the man had not been properly fertilizing a certain fig tree in a vineyard. The Lord said to me, "If men fail to do their jobs, they can open the door for the curse." He continued, "That's why I talk in Proverbs and Ecclesiastes so much about being diligent and staying busy, because if men fail to do their jobs correctly, they can open the door for something bad to happen."

In Luke 13, the keeper of the vineyard failed. It is so important to be diligent in what we do because it eliminates most of the opportunities for the curse. When people don't do what they are supposed to do, it can cause bad things to happen to good people. Scripture is plain about this.

WHOSE RESPONSIBILITY IS WHOSE?

One of the main reasons that God's answers, solutions, and cures have not been found and why mental anguish, dilemmas, and tragedies have taken place is because people are confused as to whose responsibility is whose. For example, some people blame God, Jesus, the Holy Spirit, the angels, the pastor, even the devil, for things that are *their* fault. The fact is that there are four main parties who are ultimately responsible for what happens on planet earth and to its inhabitants.

God has certain responsibilities and so do all of us. Satan, while having limits as to how far he can go, factors into the equation. He has come to kill, steal, and destroy and has left carnage in his wake. He has gained an advantage over many a soul. 2 Corinthians 2:11 says that we should not be ignorant of his devices "Lest Satan should get an advantage of us."

One of the main purposes of this book is to expose Satan and his works, and through the truth break his power of error and deception over the lives of many...even multitudes. My main goal in writing this book is to show God's purpose of victory for all of our lives and His strategy and power for bringing our victory into reality. I want to emphasize His role in causing good things to happen to us. In order to receive His purpose, strategy, and power, we must understand the sovereignty of God. I attempted to do this when I discussed my first visitation by Jesus. God does not always get His way. Millions of souls going to hell is not God getting His way. To understand this point sheds light and understanding on many *why's* in life.

Because God is omnipotent, people seem to think that nothing happens unless He allows it. Because they misunderstood His omnipotence, people have not fought back when the enemy has invaded their lives. Somehow they attributed God as being liable for bad things happening when He had nothing to do with it at all. Friends, neighbors, or loved ones were killed in car accidents and people decided that it must have been God because, after all, He didn't keep it from happening. In a twisted sense of logic, they blamed God instead of the impairment of the driver, poor maintenance of the car, or poor choices in decisions.

Man's foolishness, ignorance, and sin can temporarily and sometimes eternally thwart the plan of God. In *most* Christians' lives, God is *not* getting His way. Is this a shocking statement? We should be receiving His healing, His deliverance...His blessings. Think about it! This is not to say that Satan's power is greater than God's or anywhere near it. The truth is that the greatest problem in the church, in the world, is not the devil. "Greater is he that is in you, than he that is in the world" (1 John 4:4). The greatest problem in the church is that some Christians do not truly know their God and who they are in Him. God has power over all the power of the enemy. (Luke 10:19.)

In discussing the third reason that Jesus gave me for bad things happening to good people, we are going to factor both God and Satan out of the picture. They are only two of the four parties responsible for many of the *why's* on Earth. We are going to have to zero in on the two remaining parties of the four when we talk about diligence. These two parties are us—ourselves and other people. Our own lack of diligence and others' lack of diligence can result in bad things happening.

Why did I drown at a Christian youth camp when I was eight years old? Notice that I said that it was a *Christian* youth camp. My parents had sent me there to learn more about God. I was in an environment that was dedicated to bringing glory to God. Why did I drown? First of all, I jumped off the pier when I shouldn't have. I was negligent in my own personal safety. I wasn't being diligent to follow the rules by staying in the area designated for someone who couldn't swim. This, first and foremost, was why a bad thing happened to me that day.

Secondly, in line with Luke 13:6-9, someone else didn't do the job he was supposed to do—not like he should. Someone else was not diligent. I was just eight years old. There was a lifeguard there. There were chaperones there. All of the bases were covered if everybody was doing their jobs. But there wasn't much chaperoning going on that day. Not everyone was correctly doing his job; and because of that, the door was opened for the curse to come in. This could have cut my life short. It's entirely possible that God spoke to the girl who remembered where I was swimming. Because she listened to Him, my life was saved that day.

DILIGENCE—A CURSE-BREAKER

Jesus had something to say about diligence when He appeared to me after Angela's death. He said, "The reason I talk about diligence so much in Proverbs and Ecclesiastes is because diligence is one of the main ways that the curse can be broken. When men fail to do their job correctly and they're not diligent, they often open the door for accidents—for the curse, for bad things to happen to good people." Jesus emphasized the importance of not being slothful, but being diligent and intense for the kingdom of God. He emphasized never being lazy because laziness can open the door for the curse. Proverbs and Ecclesiastes are full of Scripture verses right along this line.

"He becometh poor that dealeth with a slack hand: but the hand of the diligent maketh rich" (Proverbs 10:4). Keep in mind that poverty doesn't have to just mean lack of finances. Deficiency comes in all shapes and sizes. We can also be deficient in mental, physical, and spiritual qualities. "The hand of the diligent shall bear rule: but the slothful shall be under tribute" (Proverbs 12:24). The Amplified Bible renders the last part of this verse: "The slothful will be put to forced labor." Lack of diligence opens the door for the enemy to force his yoke upon us in any of the categories of kill, steal, or destroy.

> *The soul of the sluggard desireth, and hath nothing: but the soul of the diligent shall be made fat.*
>
> *Proverbs 13:4*

> *A slothful man hideth his hand in his bosom, and will not so much as bring it to his mouth again.*
>
> *Proverbs 19:24*

> *The slothful hideth his hand in his bosom; it grieveth him to bring it again to his mouth.*
>
> *Proverbs 26:15*

There are those who are too lazy to feed themselves—physically, mentally, and spiritually. They will go hungry first and then they will depend on some over-responsible individual to constantly bail them out of their physical, spiritual, emotional, financial, or relational crises. They have learned to control and manipulate others to do what they should be doing. These individuals usually cry the loudest that God has failed to do what He should do, when they should be taking responsibility for themselves. Often these "slothful" individuals put themselves in a vulnerable position to be manipulated and controlled by others. Poverty puts people in this position, and poverty is a curse that is often caused by lack of diligence.

THE BIG WHY

If we don't learn to read and think for ourselves, we will be put in the vulnerable position for others to do our thinking for us. This is a curse. That's why it is so sad that young people spend so much time watching TV or DVDs, living their lives vicariously through others, instead of developing their own faculties and living out their own destinies. Laziness and lack of diligence to do what we should instead of what is convenient opens the door for the curse—an impoverished, robbed, and even destroyed destiny.

Ecclesiastes tells us there is a time to do certain things, to take care of things. We live in a world of procrastinators who put off until tomorrow what should be done today.

> *To every thing there is a season, and a time to every purpose under the heaven...a time to plant, and a time to pluck up that which is planted...a time to break down, and a time to build up...a time to rend, and a time to sew; a time to keep silence, and a time to speak.*
>
> *Ecclesiastes 3:1,2,3,7*

Timing is a major key to blessings or curses.

The bottom line is: "As the bird by wandering, as the swallow by flying, so the curse causeless shall not come" (Proverbs 26:2). When my daughter's plane crashed, men had failed to service that plane correctly. They had failed to do the required maintenance on that aircraft. Angela didn't have anything to do with it. If men fail to be diligent in their endeavors, it *can* open the door for accidents to happen to someone else.

If we know we need to get our brakes fixed on our car but we don't, then we can actually open the door for the curse. (There are people who are foolish and presumptuous enough to say that the devil "got in their brakes" when something like this happens.) We might take our car to a place where we are conned and the mechanic doesn't really fix our brakes. It's possible that something bad could happen to us because of his negligence.

I heard about a young minister who offered to do some welding for a friend inside his garage. Unbeknownst to him, the friend had spilled gasoline on his garage floor and had not cleaned up the mess. When the young minister began welding, a fire erupted, he was badly burned, and died. How many messes do we leave lying around that other people pay the consequences for? How many messes do we have to suffer for ourselves?

A young Christian girl's family physician had prescribed a drug that just wasn't doing the job. When she returned to him, he prescribed an additional drug that was never supposed to be taken in conjunction with the first drug. The warning was clearly written out for the physician's information. The young Christian girl went into a state of extreme depression, and in a matter of a few days she ended up killing herself, being completely out of her mind. She had a lovely four-year-old daughter that she practically lived for. She was a college student. She was full of dreams and aspirations and life. She would never, in her right mind, have committed suicide.

These stories are frightening and may make you feel as if you are completely at the whim of other people's failures. It feels like no matter what you do, you can still have bad things happen to you. But this is not true. Through caution, wisdom, diligence, accountability, and mature actions, we can overcome almost all of the failures of others that could potentially affect our lives. God can help us to avoid tragedy through the Holy Spirit. Many of us have heard the small, still voice inside that warns us of danger. This might feel like a minor unease or it could feel like overwhelming danger or dread. It is important to pay attention to this voice—it is God's way of protecting us from danger. "But when he, the Spirit of truth, comes, he will guide you into all truth. He will not speak on his own; he will speak only what he hears, and he will tell you what is yet to come" (John 16:13 NIV).

AWARE, FOREWARNED, AND CIRCUMSPECT

I am not sharing these stories for us to hopelessly resign ourselves to the possibility that accidents, terrible tragedies, and even death can be brought on by others failing to do their jobs. I am not suggesting this is the way it has to be. I am sharing these things so that we can be on better guard against the attacks of the enemy, and not waste our time blaming the wrong person, ourselves, or even God. Ephesians 5:15 tells us, "See then that ye walk circumspectly, not as fools, but as wise." To be informed is to be better-prepared. I could give illustration after illustration on this subject, pointing out how bad things happen to good people because of someone's lack of diligence.

Some things are out of line that we need to set straight. People have blamed everyone and everything else for things that are *their* fault. They have forgotten that the Bible says that we will reap what we sow. (Galatians 6:7.) Keep in mind we can sow good things and reap good things as well as we can sow bad things and reap bad things.

As Christians, we have a responsibility to be diligent in our lives. We have a responsibility to take care of our bodies. If we fail to dress properly in inclement weather, we can't blame the devil because we catch a cold. While we are primarily spiritual beings, we do have a body. It, for the most part, does not take care of itself. Some people say that any kind of sickness is the devil's fault. While sickness does lead back to Satan and the curse, we still have a responsibility to be good stewards of our body. We can willfully walk out from under God's protection through sin, foolishness, and ignorance. While nothing can separate us from the love of God, because of our free will and a lack of knowledge we can choose to walk out from under God's divine protection.

Know ye not, that to whom ye yield yourselves servants to obey,
his servants ye are to whom ye obey; whether of sin unto death, or
of obedience unto righteousness.

Romans 6:16

When we willfully walk out from God's protection, we give the devil a "legal" door of entry. We are not innocent victims. In such cases, it is foolish or presumptuous to believe that no bad thing will "come nigh our dwelling." (Psalm 91:10.) This is not to say that we cannot repent and change, but let's save ourselves possibly a world of hurt by not going this far.

We must understand that if Satan gets the opportunity to kill a believer, he will. He will do so with great delight, because the only believer that he likes is a dead one. There are some Christians who have opened themselves up to be taken out of this world by the devil. We have been wrong to say that the devil took them, because in reality it was their fault. It is different when the enemy wrongfully spills innocent blood. According to what the Lord told me that night He visited me, people often experience bad things because of lack of diligence, even the loss of life.

I would venture to say that when Christians are experiencing negative situations, it is *usually* because someone has failed to do his or her job correctly. One of the most obvious examples of this is within marriage. God instituted marriage before He instituted the Church, and marriages lead to more humans being born who are potential members of the family of God. Satan hates the family of God and viciously attacks individual families within it. I want to address how failing to do our jobs diligently as husbands or wives has opened the door to allow the enemy to waltz in and destroy a marriage. "Tupperware Versus China" is a message within a message about diligence.

TUPPERWARE VERSUS CHINA

Why do marriages fall apart? Usually someone—the husband, the wife, or both—has failed to do the right thing. In a husband and wife relationship, Peter says, "Likewise, ye husbands, dwell with them [your wives] according to knowledge, giving honour unto the wife as unto the weaker vessel, and as being heirs together of the grace of life; that your prayers be not hindered" (1 Peter 3:7). Peter says that the husband should see himself and his wife "as being heirs together of the grace of life." They should see, love, and treat each other as a brother and sister in the family of God. This means to do what Paul says in Romans 12:10, "Be kindly affectioned one to another with brotherly love; in honour preferring one another."

One of the most unique statements Peter ever made was to say that the husband and wife should see each other "as being heirs together of the grace of life." Most husbands and wives do not prefer one another as members of the body of Christ—not like they should. They see each other based only upon an aspect of their relationship, leaving this one out. As a result, one or both of them does his or her job incorrectly.

They do not apply their relationship correctly; they do not truly prefer one another.

The Scripture says for the husband to give "honour unto the wife as unto the weaker vessel." Think of this in terms of the difference between Tupperware and china. Allow me to use an analogy. Let's take a Tupperware container and a china cup. Both of them have the same volume and are capable of holding the same amount of coffee or tea. But one is a "weaker" vessel, meaning that it has to be handled more delicately than the other.

Men are like Tupperware, and women are like china. Both can perform similar functions, to a degree, but their presentation or expression of that function can be completely different. Quite frankly, that's the way it should be, but such differences can pose a challenge. If not perceived correctly, these differences can result in a deeper rift rather than constructing a bridge in the husband-wife relationship. My point is that emotionally, physically, and spiritually there's a difference between men and women, between husbands and wives. It's not a matter of quantity—one being of greater capacity; it's a matter of quality—and, that too, is not implying that one is greater and the other lesser. If husbands fail to recognize this, they can open the door for bad things to happen. Many times men treat women emotionally or verbally like they would other men. Likewise, some women treat men as if they are women. Then misunderstandings occur. We walk away from each other saying, "I just don't understand that person. It makes sense to me, and yet it makes no sense to him (or her) whatsoever." The fact is that men and women have been created fundamentally different. A man should never relate to a woman emotionally and verbally like he would relate to another man and then expect her to respond like a woman, and vice versa.

The difference between Tupperware and fine china is that even though both may hold the same amount, one of them is a finer, more fragile vessel. To me the problems of male/female misunderstandings can be dealt with through this simple illustration. Tupperware is tough and coarse, but fine china is fragile. Men are like Tupperware, and women are like fine china. Men, like Tupperware, can take many more bumps along the way. Women, like china, need to be handled with care. God didn't say that men are superior to women. Women can think, talk, reason, and do everything else just as well as men can—often better. What God did say is that she is a *finer* vessel, and the problem today is that many men are dropping their "china." They are not being diligent and doing their jobs correctly.

"HE SAYS, SHE SAYS"

The differences between the genders can actually make marriages stronger. Generally, men tend to think logically about things, whereas women tend to think emotionally. This can lead to better decision-making. For instance, when Cindy and I first got married, I sold my Chevy Vega, got a good job, and purchased a Pontiac Grand LeMans. I had just left the Air Force, and I really wanted this car! It was the finest maroon-colored Grand LeMans ever made, with a 400xy super-charged engine, dual glass packs, dual exhausts, a white vinyl top, white interior and black carpet. Brother, it was hot—and it purred like a kitten!

I'll never forget the day I drove the car home, and Cindy said, "I want another car." Man, I just knew the honeymoon was over!

"You what? You want another car? This is the fastest, hottest-running car anywhere around here! This car is beautiful. It has a white interior; it's got a powerful engine. Why?" I asked.

"I don't like the way it sounds," she replied.

So, I got another car! Why? Because it wasn't just *my* car. It was *our* car, and the hot rod *boom* under the hood embarrassed the *other owner.*

Another difference between men and women is that men tend to come across as rather indifferent and impersonal, while women tend to take things more personally. Men need to understand what makes women tick so they can understand their responses. And ladies, when a man zones out, it doesn't necessarily mean he's mean and insensitive. Generally speaking, we're just not as emotionally involved with things that don't personally affect us.

Men also tend to be very goal-oriented in life, whereas women tend to be more relationship-oriented. Men are success-oriented while women are security-minded. He says, "I'm going to take everything out of the savings account and invest it in this business plan. It's all or nothing, Babe. What do you say?"

"You pull one penny out of there, and you're dead meat!" she replies. The maternal instinct kicks in. She's watched her husband blow his money for years, so she wants to make sure they have enough money to feed the kids next week.

Women tend to need roots—they need a house, a place to call their own. They need a place where they can feel secure, and they like it kept a certain way. There is a measure of security in the way things are kept.

Men just walk into the house "as is." Some ladies have to literally house-train their husbands. Their insensitive clods walk in with grease or mud on the bottom of their shoes and track it all over the carpet. Forget the fact that you have to steam-clean carpets these days. Then the guys look back and say, "I didn't do that. My shoes did it." Just because he's a soup brain, ladies, doesn't mean it's time to get a divorce. It's simply time to understand there are some basic differences. Both the husband and the wife need to deal with these differences in an intelligent, godly, loving way. Embracing our differences and understanding our roles in the marriage can lead to good things happening in the relationship. This is why the Apostle Peter says for husbands and wives to "dwell together" according to *knowledge*, not just according to *nature*. (1 Peter 3:7.)

PROPHET, PRIEST, AND KING

When we discover who Jesus is, we discover who we should be in our home, but many men don't want to live like Christ. They don't want to love their family like Christ does. They want to do their own thing, be their own man—come home, sleep, eat, drink, get up and leave, and turn in a paycheck once a week.

God promised He will never leave you, He will never forsake you. He will be with you always. (Deuteronomy 31:6.) Men, if we haven't absorbed that mentality, then we need to renew our minds regarding family relationships. Much of our wife's strength comes from us. Much of our children's stability—mentally, socially and financially—comes from us. When men don't fulfill their rightful roles, their children can grow up rebellious, insecure, and emotionally fragile. Failure to be diligent in relationship responsibility is one of the main reasons why the curse can come upon families

Contrary to popular belief, we aren't called to be a *boss* in our home but a *priest*. We may say, "I'm the boss of my house, and a man's home is his castle," but we are we setting ourselves up for a fall! We're not the boss in our house. We are representatives of Christ in our home. Christ led by serving, not demanding, and there is a big difference. We should instigate love in our homes, in our words, and in our deeds. Can you see the difference that understanding our correct role can make? What would marriage be like if we diligently worked to serve like Christ?

MARRIAGE COMES WITH A SET OF INSTRUCTIONS

We have a home computer that came with all the bells and whistles. Not being very computer savvy, one day I really messed up. I was playing the only thing I knew how to play on it—golf! Just as I was about to shoot par, the computer died on me, and I couldn't get the golf game to come back up. Now, I don't know how to fix a computer, but I got in there and acted like an IBM repairman. I turned every switch on and off. I punched the enter key, the delete key, the escape key—all the keys. I thought, *Well, if it blows up, I'll be no worse off.*

Finally, a friend came over and started doing things by the instruction manual. A click here and a click there, and in three minutes he had the computer running again. Up came the golf game on the screen, and Arnold Palmer and I started down the fairway again.

That's a good example of what happens with married couples. They don't use the instruction manual. They are not diligent to follow the guidelines. So they blindly start trying to fix their relationship with their own ideas of what might work, *and they only make things worse.* These ideas are often self-justifying or self-serving. They can be shallow, seemingly insincere efforts to deal with very deep, serious issues. Our marriage is from heaven. It's not carnal—it's supernatural. If we start tinkering with our marriage without the proper instructions, we're going to mess things up—just like I did with our computer. We need to play the game by the rules in order for it to work. The first rule is this: "Husbands, love your wives, even as Christ also loved the church" (Ephesians 5:25).

Husbands and wives need to learn to ask why the other is hurting. Hurts are emotional and they can be long-lasting. We should never say things like, "I don't understand that woman. Every time I turn around, she's crying over something. I don't understand."

I once heard about a guy who was watching a football game on television. His wife was in the kitchen slicing vegetables when she cut her finger and started hollering, "Oh my! Oh my! I'm hurt! I'm hurt!"

The guy just sat there, watching television. She was screaming, "Oh, my finger is cut. I cut my finger!"

Finally the guy snapped out of it, ran to her, and said, "Dear God, I thought I was going deaf."

That's the way some husbands listen to their wives, but it doesn't have to be that way. Bitter and sweet water can't flow out of the same vessel, but Tupperware and china can complement one another. Husbands and wives must decide to be kind and tenderhearted towards each other. One of our highest priorities in our lives should be making our households a place of love and peace—Tupperware and china reflecting God's best, holding to and doing what God fashioned them to do.

We must learn to forgive one another by being able to see our *own* faults. If we can see our own faults and weaknesses, we will never have trouble forgiving our spouse. As long as we are trying to prove we're right, however, we can't be a person of forgiveness.

BECAUSE OF LACK OF DILIGENCE

Part of overcoming the negative *why's* in a marriage is by relating to our spouse through edifying communication. Ephesians 5:4 warns about filthiness, foolish talking, and jesting. Foolish jesting is insensitive joking. Men, for instance, don't pick on your wife about her weight when you know it hurts her. Ladies, don't joke about his receding hairline when he really can't do anything about it. Don't run down your mother-in-law when you know it causes a problem. There are often areas that people joke about that in actuality hurt deeply. Although it may be a big joke to us, another wound can be opened—and the scar will remain. Support and love each other. Speaking positively about sensitive subjects in a home is a true key to overcoming the *why's* of disunity.

I've already said that when Christians are experiencing negative situations, it is usually because someone has failed to do his or her job correctly. I will go further to say that when people are experiencing negative situations in marriage, it is usually because the husband, wife, or both have failed to do their job correctly. Someone has caused bad things to happen in their lives or someone else's because of lack of diligence. This can usually explain many of the relational *why's*.

Chapter 9

BECAUSE OF EVIL SPIRITS

The Lord next took me to verses 10 and 11 of Luke, chapter 13: "And he was teaching in one of the synagogues on the sabbath. And, behold, there was a woman which had a spirit of infirmity eighteen years, and was bowed together, and could in no wise lift up herself." This woman had a demon of sickness—a spirit of infirmity.

The Lord told me, "The fourth reason that bad things can happen is because of demon spirits." He added that it was significant that this woman had the infirmity for *eighteen* years and that there had been *eighteen* men at the tower of Siloam. The number "eighteen" was a tie between these two incidents: two reasons out of the four that the Lord revealed from Luke 13 as to why bad things happen to people, including good people.

Our Father wants us to know the truth and He wants it to be easy to find. Of wisdom, He says in Proverbs 1, "She crieth in the chief place of concourse, in the openings of the gates: in the city she uttereth her words" (v. 21). "She cries at the head of the noisy intersections [in the chief gathering places]; at the entrance of the city gates she speaks" (v.21 AMP). God wants us to hear His voice. He wants to make His message simple and available, so He is not hiding it in dark alleys or up lonely hollows. He is crying it in the open, in chief gathering places, where it is easily accessed. What's more, He will use simple, everyday illustrations, and familiar things to get it across—like coins, bread, stones, fish, candles, birds of the air, and lilies of the field.

For my family and for the body of Christ, Jesus gave me this message. He put it all together in one chapter and used the number "eighteen" twice to show that He was connecting these thoughts to get an urgent and vital word to His people. This may have been a small gesture on His part, but it was a special touch on our behalf. Sometimes the small things speak the loudest, because they show His attention to the details in our lives. Sometimes that can speak more loudly of His love for us than the big things He does.

We can take one of these four reasons—cults and bad government, the curse, lack of diligence, or evil spirits—and explain why most bad things happen, like the unexplained accident that results in death. Cults or bad government could be responsible for the martyrdom of a child of God. How do we explain James, the brother of John, getting beheaded, but not Peter? We have two men here who both love Jesus, who both walked with Jesus. One of them gets his head cut off and the other one doesn't. Did God love Peter more than He loved John? No, it had nothing to do with that. In this case, it had to do with a cult (Judaizers who were mixing the law with grace) and bad government, but it also had to do with the curse and evil spirits. All four of the reasons for bad things happening to good people can be intertwined. For example, evil spirits have instigated and helped propagate cults, have inspired bad governments, and have had their part in carrying out the curse.

THE POWER OF EVIL SPIRITS

In the Bible we are told that one third of the angels were cast out of heaven with Satan when Satan was thrown down to the earth. The angels that fell with Lucifer and were cast out of heaven are a class of fallen spirit beings called demons or devils—evil spirits.

These evil spirits attack, torment, and even dominate a person in a number of ways.

First of all, you need to know that a Christian cannot be demon-possessed. Possession implies ownership. A Christian has been redeemed, purchased by the blood of Christ, and he belongs to God. His spirit is now the home of the Spirit of God. The Spirit of God that lives in the spirit of the Christian cannot cohabit with a demon. I pointed out in the chapter "Because of the Curse" that one of the saddest errors in present church teaching is that people who are saved and filled with the Holy Spirit can also be demon possessed. This is not true. Christians who *seem* to be demon possessed simply have never been delivered from the power of iniquity.

The Christian has indeed been delivered "from the power [the control, dominion, or authority] of darkness" (Colossians 1:13). However, if a person allows for the existence of darkness through negativity, immorality, sin, or simply no faith, he leaves himself open and susceptible to demonic assault—both in his soul and physically. He has given the enemy an open and legal door of entry into his life. While a Christian's spirit is awakened to God and set free, the mind still needs to be renewed and the body still needs to be brought under subjection. These two things take a longer time to accomplish.

The thought-life, for example, needs cleansing and training with the Word of God. Some people have thoughts that tend towards evil. This can give the enemy a *strong* hold in their lives. These are the *strongholds* that Paul talks about in 2 Corinthians 10:4 that need to be pulled down. In order to pull down these strongholds, we have to recognize and believe the truth of the Bible and replace wrong thoughts with

God's truth. Evil spirits can be comfortably situated in strongholds in our lives that we have built with thoughts that are unlike God's. The Apostle Paul, in 2 Corinthians 10:5, tells us how to pull down these strongholds. He calls it "casting down imaginations, and every high thing that exalteth itself against the knowledge of God, and bringing into captivity every thought to the obedience of Christ."

Our un-transformed thoughts can give way to what is called *oppression* by demons. While evil spirits cannot possess us, they can impose themselves upon us, burdening us, restraining us, and exercising authority in our lives if we have allowed them to do so.

A powerful, yet confusing verse, is found in 1 John 5:18, which says, "We know that whosoever is born of God sinneth not; but he that is begotten of God keepeth himself, and that wicked one toucheth him not." Someone who is born of God will not deliberately and knowingly practice sin as a way of life. But notice in particular that this verse says that he "keepeth himself, and that wicked one toucheth him not." *Keeping ourselves* by committing our thought life to God is essential because the wicked one will not be able to get a grip on us. This can easily explain the *why's* of some effects of evil spirits in people's lives. We are responsible for *keeping ourselves*, just as this was pointed out when we talked about reason three, "Because of the Lack of Diligence."

Satan, who is the father of lies, sends forth his lying, deceiving spirits to start false doctrines. Because they spread these false doctrines, cults are instrumental in causing wrong patterns of thinking in the lives of people. These wrong thoughts can tend to become more important than the knowledge of God. Therefore, wrong patterns of thinking give liberty to evil spirits to oppress people. This is an intermeshing of these two reasons—cults and evil spirits—for causing bad things to happen to good people. Though this is a very deep, sensitive topic because it deals with such an unfamiliar subject matter (evil spirits), it nonetheless can often be the key to *why* some things occur in life.

The devil wars against our minds and bodies, and he tries to beat us down spiritually, as well. We have to strengthen our hearts and minds by praying like Jude 20 tells us to: "But ye, beloved, building up yourselves on your most holy faith, praying in the Holy Ghost." While it is true that we cannot be demon-possessed, we can be *oppressed* by evil spirits. They can find a place of habitation in our soul and body, with the real battlefield being the mind.

VARIOUS CAPACITIES OF EVIL SPIRITS

Demons seek habitation, preferably human. When Jesus cast the legion of devils out of the demoniac of Gadara, they had such a desire for embodiment that they "besought him [Jesus], saying, Send us into the swine, that we may enter them" (Mark 5:12). Certainly demons working through a human being can accomplish more damage than working through an animal. That's why demons seek human habitation. "When the unclean spirit is gone out of a man, he walketh through dry places, seeking rest, and findeth none. Then he saith, I will return into my house from whence I came out" (Matthew 12:43-44).

Just as the talents and abilities of human beings greatly vary, so do the evil talents and abilities of demons. Many kinds of evil spirits are mentioned in the Bible: blind, deaf, deceiving, seducing, jealous, insane, familiar, and others. Deceiving, jealous, and seducing spirits afflict the soul.

Deceiving Spirits. Deceiving or lying spirits are often mentioned in the Bible. The wicked king of Israel and husband to Jezebel was at war with Syria. His time of judgment had come. An evil spirit—a lying spirit—came forth to bring about his demise.

> *And the LORD said, Who shall persuade Ahab, that he may go up*
> *and fall at Ramoth gilead? And one said on this manner, and*
> *another said on that manner. And there came forth a spirit...and*
> *said, I will go forth, and I will be a lying spirit in the mouth of*
> *all his prophets.*
>
> *1 Kings 22:20-22*

Even though lying spirits are of Satan (Ahab was an instrument of Satan as well), the devil has no allegiance to his own.

Jealous Spirits & Spirits of Betrayal. When Saul did not fully carry out God's orders against the Amalekites in 1 Samuel 15, his disobedience brought the disfavor of God. Instead of repenting, Saul became jealous and suspicious of others who he feared would usurp his throne.

> *The very next day, a tormenting spirit from God overwhelmed*
> *Saul...David was playing the harp, as he did each day. But Saul*
> *had a spear in his hand, and he suddenly hurled it at David,*
> *intending to pin him to the wall. But David escaped him twice.*
> *Saul was then afraid of David, for the LORD was with David, and*
> *had turned away from Saul.*
>
> *1 Samuel 18:10-12 NLT*

Bad things have happened, even to very good people, because of a jealous and traitorous spirit. We can allow ourselves to become

BECAUSE OF EVIL SPIRITS

wrongly ambitious. We can allow fear—fear that others will be more successful than we are—to dictate our behavior rather than God and His Word. We can strategize to keep our positions and to keep others from coming to our level or worse, getting ahead of us. Or we can try to take a position that belongs to someone else—not to us. These types of thoughts can sometimes begin with demonic thinking that creates a stronghold for a spirit of jealousy and betrayal. Unfortunately, this kind of thinking could lead to the social and emotional "murdering" of brothers, sisters, or friends—using gossip and betrayal to destroy their reputations or to make their endeavors difficult.

In the Bible there is a man named Abimelech who usurped the throne of Israel and murdered seventy of his brethren in the process. Because he opened the door with his murderous deed, God allowed an evil spirit to incite betrayal and rebellion against him. God allowed an evil spirit to come between Abimelech and the men of Shechem. (Judges 9:22-24.)

Seducing Spirits. We could call these "religious demons." They are capable of persuasively leading people into cults and false religions, and they will find wrongly ambitious people particularly easy prey. A person's own pride and conceit can make him a prime target for some false revelation that builds his ego and makes him overconfident of his spirituality. " Now the Spirit speaketh expressly, that in the latter times some shall depart from the faith, giving heed to seducing spirits, and doctrines of devils" (1 Timothy 4:1).

Deaf and Blind Spirits. Demons have the capability of affecting or exercising control over specific organs of the body and nerve centers: auditory, optic, vocal, and spinal. "When Jesus saw that the people came running together, he rebuked the foul spirit, saying unto him, Thou dumb and deaf spirit, I charge thee, come out of him, and enter no more into him" (Mark 9:25). "Then was brought unto him one possessed with a devil, blind, and dumb: and he healed him, insomuch that the blind and dumb both spake and saw" (Matthew 12:22).

Spirits of infirmity. A spirit of infirmity can affect the body in various ways. It can cause a person's body to be twisted or bowed over so he cannot lift himself up, just like the woman in Luke 13:11, "which had a spirit of infirmity eighteen years, and was bowed together, and could in no wise lift up herself." This is certainly not to imply that all infirm people have demons in their lives. However, the root cause of all sickness and infirmity is from the curse in operation and its continuing effects in the earth.

THE SPIRIT OF RELIGION

Without a doubt, one of the greatest causes of *why* in the world is a spirit of false religion. The spirit of religion deserves a little further elaboration because it may be the most dangerous, deadliest spirit of all. We have already discussed this spirit (without addressing it as a spirit and without calling it a spirit of religion) under cults and bad governments and curses.

We can say without reservation that Satan is religious. He's not a Christian and he is not holy, *but he is religious and very spiritual.* He became the devil in an effort to be like God. Power, not the holy nature of God, is what he wanted.

How art thou fallen from heaven, O Lucifer, son of the morning! how art thou cut down to the ground, which didst weaken the nations! For thou hast said in thine heart, I will ascend into heaven, I will exalt my throne above the stars of God: I will sit

also upon the mount of the congregation, in the sides of the north:
I will ascend above the heights of the clouds; I will be like the
most High.

Isaiah 14:12-14

Ezekiel, chapter 28, sheds some more light on who the devil is
to help us understand why the spirit of religion is perhaps his *most*
powerful tool:

Son of man, take up a lamentation upon the king of Tyrus, and
say unto him, Thus saith the Lord GOD; Thou sealest up the sum,
full of wisdom, and perfect in beauty. Thou hast been in Eden
the garden of God; every precious stone was thy covering, the
sardius, topaz, and the diamond, the beryl, the onyx, and the
jasper, the sapphire, the emerald, and the carbuncle, and gold: the
workmanship of thy tabrets and of thy pipes was prepared in thee
in the day that thou wast created. Thou art the anointed cherub
that covereth; and I have set thee so: thou wast upon the holy
mountain of God; thou hast walked up and down in the midst
of the stones of fire. Thou wast perfect in thy ways from the day
that thou wast created, till iniquity was found in thee. By the
multitude of thy merchandise they have filled the midst of thee
with violence, and thou hast sinned: therefore I will cast thee
as profane out of the mountain of God: and I will destroy thee,
O covering cherub, from the midst of the stones of fire. Thine
heart was lifted up because of thy beauty, thou hast corrupted thy
wisdom by reason of thy brightness: I will cast thee to the ground,
I will lay thee before kings, that they may behold thee.

Ezekiel 28:12-17

THE BIG WHY

The devil knows something firsthand about wisdom, beauty, the anointing, holiness, and then a heart that is lifted up in pride and wisdom that is corrupted. He used to walk "upon the holy mountain of God…in the midst of the stones of fire" (v.14).

I said that Satan is religious. He continues to desire to be God, or at least "a god" deserving of the worship of the universe. He knows that man is a spiritual being with an inherent need to worship God. We have already said that there is a pure and undefiled religion in the service and worship of the God of the Bible. What Satan has attempted is not to deny religion, but to pervert it. He tries to direct man's worship toward him, the devil, as he hides behind many guises—even forms of Christianity.

The greatest deception is a church that is controlled by a religious spirit. Within the church, the devil uses legalism to distract God's people from the reality of Christ's salvation. We will have to be on guard against the religious spirit in days to come.

PART FOUR

THE
THIRD
VISITATION

THEIR WORKS WILL FOLLOW

And I heard a voice from heaven saying unto me, Write, Blessed
are the dead which die in the Lord from henceforth: Yea, saith the
Spirit, that they may rest from their labours; and their works do
follow them.

Revelation 14:13

In the Lord's third visit that night, He talked about how my daughter's works would follow her according to Revelation 14:13: "The dead which die in the Lord...rest from their labours, and their works do follow them"—I didn't understand that. I didn't understand how to bring Angela's works forward, but I came to understand that Angela's works would continue, following her departure. I would have something to do with making that happen.

Today the message of Revelation 14:13 is demonstrated through Angela's ongoing ministry. Her works are following her; they are still going on though she rests in the presence of God from her labors on earth.

Chapter 10

EVEN MORE AND GREATER

The great cloud of witnesses in Hebrews provides an excellent scriptural example of "their works [did] follow them." Those in the Hebrews 11, "Hall of Fame" greatly pleased God, and were even put into the category "of whom the world was not worthy" (Hebrews 11:38). God's promises to this group were not just the promises of heaven, but promises in the earth. Proverbs 11:31 says it this way: "The righteous shall be recompensed [or rewarded] in the earth." Yet, the Word talks about promises that the righteous did not get to personally directly receive in this lifetime. Hebrews 11:39-40 and Hebrews 12:1 point this out:

And these all, having obtained a good report through faith, received not the promise: God having provided some better thing for us, that they without us should not be made perfect. Wherefore seeing we also are compassed about with so great a cloud of witnesses...

While these righteous people did not directly receive their blessings while here on earth, their blessings are still "recompensed *in the earth*" (emphasis mine) to those who remain. God made promises to Angela and others, who, like her, walked uprightly before Him. These promises were not released in their lifetimes but were to be released at a future time to those who came after them. We become the beneficiaries of what they sowed. They sowed and others will get to reap what they sowed. The beneficiaries will receive from and even continue their works, carrying them forward to *something even more and greater.* To this extent, Angela is still accruing rewards here on earth while she is in heaven.

It's like when Jesus said that "the works that I do shall he [the believer] do also; and greater works than these shall he [the believer] do; because I go unto my Father" (John 14:12). Because Jesus went to the Father, something even greater was able to take place on the earth.

Isaiah says of Jesus, "He had done no violence, neither was any deceit in his mouth" (Isaiah 53:9). One of the thieves who was crucified along with Jesus said in Luke 23:41, "But this man hath done nothing amiss." 2 Corinthians 5:21 says, "For he hath made him to be sin for us, who knew no sin." Jesus' crucifixion was the shedding of *innocent* blood. This was a price that had to be paid and was ordained of God from the very beginning—"And all that dwell upon the earth shall worship him, whose names are not written in the book *of life of the Lamb slain from the foundation of the world*" (Revelations 13:8, emphasis mine). Before the problem of man's sinfulness even existed, God had the solution. That's the way He is. Before there is a question, He has the answer. Before there is a disease, He has the cure.

So the princes of this world crucified Jesus, thinking they had won. But 1 Corinthians 2:8 tells us that if had they understood God's plan, they would not have killed Jesus—"for had they known it, they would not have crucified the Lord of glory." Not only was the price paid for man's sin, but the Spirit of God was sent to live inside every believer to empower him to do the works of Jesus and even "greater works." The Holy Spirit that descended upon Jesus at the time of His water baptism, right before His earthly ministry took off, was now released to reside in every believer. When Jesus was crucified, God bestowed His mantle upon the body of Christ, just as Elijah had bestowed his mantle upon Elisha. The enemy had no idea that a recompense was coming when he crucified Jesus. He had no idea that the works of Jesus were to follow and be even greater.

No one else has been called to shed his blood for the sins of the world. But the enemy has wrongfully and prematurely taken servants of God—martyrs, aborted babies, or God's people both young and old. These people had not opened the door to give Satan a legal right to their lives, and the fact remains that Jesus recompenses. When people die in the work of the Lord, they are called martyrs, and God never lets a martyr die without a response. Jesus said that He would repay. The works of those unjustly taken will follow. They will be recompensed in the earth.

> *Instead of your [former] shame you shall have a twofold recompense; instead of dishonor and reproach [your people] shall rejoice in their portion. Therefore in their land they shall possess double [what they had forfeited]; everlasting joy shall be theirs.*
> *Isaiah 61:7 AMP*

> *For I the Lord love justice; I hate robbery and wrong with violence…And I will faithfully give them their recompense in truth, and I will make an everlasting covenant or league with them.*
> *Isaiah 61:8 AMP*

> *Men do not despise a thief, if he steal to satisfy his soul when he is hungry; but if he be found, he shall restore sevenfold; he shall give all the substance of his house.*
> *Proverbs 6:30-31*

Angela's Works

Angela is being "recompensed in the earth," here and now, as her works do follow and are carried forward. This book itself is part of the fulfilling of God's word to me that her works would follow, and that I would have a role in this.

An Anointing to be Transferred

Angela's legacy is one of contagious energy and deeply intense passion that will continue to stir and feed the stories, ministries, and destinies of others. Her works have already been following, and will continue forever, as many will be in heaven because of her investment in their lives.

There was a call of God upon my daughter's life and a specific anointing given to her for fulfilling that call. She glorified God with her life, and her life personified what God wanted to say to a generation. She let her generation know that Jesus is alive. I believe that part of the recompense involves many others who will desire and seek after the anointing of the Holy Spirit because of what they saw Angela do for the glory of God. Only God knows how many have already been and will continue to be infected by Angela's energy and fervent passion for her God and His work.

There was a call on Angela's life for this day and hour that will be imparted to her generation. This reminds me of the first time the Lord spoke to me about recompensing and how the works of those who were "robbed" would follow them. He said, "The reason that I had the coats of those who were stoning Stephen laid at the feet of Saul of Tarsus was to signify that the mantle of Stephen had fallen back down on Saul, who became Apostle Paul. Paul would now assume responsibility for these people hearing the word of God, for bringing forward not only what God told him to do, but Stephen's works also."

EVANGELISTIC FERVOR AND EFFORTS INTENSIFIED

Angela was the Junior High Youth Pastor at our church. She founded her youth church on 1 Peter 2:9 from the *Message Bible*:

But you are the ones chosen by God, chosen for the high calling of priestly work, chosen to be a holy people, God's instruments to do his work and speak out for him, to tell others of the night-and-day difference he made for you—from nothing to something, from rejected to accepted.

Because of this, Angela named our youth church The Chosen.

It was very important to her that the ministry be called a youth *church* and not a youth *group*. To Angela, "group" sounded like a group of people meeting for a small purpose with no forward motion or vision. A youth *church*, on the other hand, is a group of young people who have vision, worship God, and minister to people. Angela stressed this concept to her teens and volunteer staff.

This purpose and vision for our youth church has carried over all these years, as has its name, The Chosen. It reaches hundreds of teens every week through school lunches, Bible clubs, youth church services, drama, dance, praise and worship, media, outreach, counseling, and social media. Several discipleship classes are done annually in addition to mission trips and summer camp.

THE BIG WHY

Jennifer, our youngest daughter, shared at Angela's Homegoing Celebration that her sister's ability to organize a youth church will be one of her greatest legacies. She pointed out that the church congregation can continue youth church because Angela revealed her goals to the church members so clearly. "I believe we knew her heart well enough to walk through her plans," Jennifer stated.

Angela determined to have the best youth church and the best youth building for the junior high kids in our area. She very carefully considered the building and the money that would be needed. When she addressed The Chosen just a few days before the accident, she sounded like a seasoned, adult pastor speaking to a large congregation of men and women who were about to take on the task of building some mega-million-dollar structure as she challenged the junior high boys and girls that night:

> He [God] desires that you be blessed, that's why He makes it so simple. It doesn't matter how much you give, but that you give. Giving isn't just in money; it's in time and effort. It's in relationship. It's in whatever can be given.
>
> God gave Jesus as His Son, and what did He get in return? The whole world...right? Or every person who becomes a Christian.
>
> I think it is so incredible it absolutely blows my mind, blows my mind when I think about in the Bible all the stories, all the stories that we've heard a billion and one times about giving and receiving. Things we've heard so many times that we tend to blow them off; but they're divine principles that work in us day in and day out in life... every day.

See, God made everything in the Bible easy. He didn't make anything difficult. If He had made giving and receiving difficult, nobody would be able to do it. But it's so simple, so simple. That's the way it works. That's why God put it in the Bible. That's why He has people teach it, because God desires that you be blessed…all of us. That's why He made it so simple.

So from now on make a decision. Make a decision that you'll never let the offering bucket pass you by without putting something in there. I don't care what it is. If it's a penny, a dollar, three dollars. God doesn't look at what you give but at your actions.

He's happy to see you happy. He's happy to see you blessed. The Bible says that He supplies all our needs according to His riches in glory by Christ Jesus. When we give, He gives back to us. And what I want you to get out of this tonight is that it's so simple to be blessed. It's so easy to have the blessings of God flowing in your life and through your life, in you and out of you.

The Bible says that God will open up the windows of heaven and pour out a blessing on us that is so vast that we don't even have room to receive it. And when I think about it and I think about God, how can I have so much blessing that I don't even have room enough to receive it? How can I have so much that I don't know what to do with it?… I can promise you that He will; the Bible says He will. And I give faithfully, I tithe, and I offer just like you do.

So for each of us who tithe and offer faithfully, I firmly believe that this year we will see the blessings of God and the windows of heaven opened up and we'll have poured out onto us so much that we don't even have room to receive it...individually as well as at The Chosen. You all, we've got a lot to do this year. We have a lot of people to reach. We have a lot of stuff to build. We have a lot to buy. We've got a lot of people to get saved. And it takes money.

When I come to The Chosen, I'm going to put something in the offering every time it passes me by. What you get back from God will be so much greater than what you give so that you'll have a real revelation of how easy it is to be blessed.

Angela did not stop with her sermon that night. She asked for a commitment from her congregation of young teenage boys and girls. She asked them to stand if they would put something in the offering every time it was passed in youth service in the coming year. I don't believe one boy or girl was left seated. She was only seventeen, but she took the work of God so seriously. Angela's life was not full of years, but her years were full of life...full of power and grace in obedience to Jesus.

"Out of the mouth of babes and sucklings hast thou ordained strength because of thine enemies, that thou mightiest still the enemy and the avenger" (Psalm 8:2). These "babes," according to the *Message Bible*, "drown out enemy talk, and silence atheist babble." That was and continues to be Angela.

The day she went to be with the Lord, she was on her way to look at a youth facility that would attract teenagers. Our church carried out that goal by creating a facility complete with an indoor skate park, video game room, three on-three basketball cage, theater, café, pool tables, air hockey tables, live band, and seating capacity for several hundred. It has been the attraction we needed to compel teens to come to youth church, be ministered to, and learn that living for God is full of fun. Angela's works were brought forward—they follow her.

Catherine, my oldest daughter, shared at Angela's Homegoing Celebration as well, saying that her younger sister would never give up on people that she, Catherine, would cast aside as unredeemable. Angela would pray sometimes until midnight for people: "She was always caring. She'd always go for the person who was out on the edge that you thought wasn't going to quite make it. And I'd say, 'Angela, would you just leave that person alone…you've prayed yourself blue in the face.' And she'd say, 'Catherine, you need compassion.'"

Angela's evangelistic fervor and efforts were not snuffed out when that plane crashed—no more than Stephen's death squelched the spread of Christianity, but rather resulted in a scattering of the church which sent its members "every where preaching the word" (Acts 8:1,4).

"The Road to Emmaus." The day before Angela's fateful flight, she was finalizing plans for the Easter production at our church that year. She met with her mother and me for at least two hours at a restaurant. She had finished her college classes for the day, and she joined me and Cindy at Papa Seafood. That was the day before Cindy's birthday. Angela went to heaven on her mother's birthday.

Angela had written out all of the scenes for the play, which she had pulled from the Gospels. She had the two men on the road to Emmaus, and they were carrying on all this dialogue; she had all these literary sketches or vignettes in the works. She was discussing with her mother and me how she wanted the play to be carried out. I had some specific ideas that I thought were pretty good, and every now and then I would try to interject something. Angela graciously listened to my ideas, but then proceeded to tell me how it was going to happen according to her plan. She was not interested in my suggestions, though she never let me know—at least not personally.

When Cindy talked about this luncheon at Angela's Homegoing Celebration, she remembered Angela biting her lip as she listened to my ideas that day. Following the lunch, when Cindy and Angela drove home together, Cindy said that Angela joked, "Poor Dad. He just doesn't understand drama. He tries so hard, but he just doesn't understand."

We went on to call that play "The Road to Emmaus," and it is now our annual Easter production. It has two hundred cast members in it, and Angela wrote the whole thing. It's full of live animals, including camels. It's a major production; it's not a little thing—and every year hundreds of people in attendance get saved.

"Heartbreak Hotel, Hotel Hallelujah." Then there is the play, "Heartbreak Hotel, Hotel Hallelujah," that I talked about earlier in the book—a live extravaganza featuring celebrity impersonators, animals, bands, and more. In its three-month run the year before Angela went home, it drew more than thirty thousand attendees and resulted in some three thousand people committing their lives to Jesus.

It was Angela's play—she brought it to La Marque. It was originally produced by Dr. Steve Muncey, but she adapted it with her "Angela" touch. We have done it almost every year since she left. It was performed one year with her, and then she went to heaven. In the production, Angela performed a lip-sync routine as the lead singer of the Dixie Chicks. She was seventeen years old and doing all of this. It was her play; she did it.

From these two plays alone—"The Road to Emmaus" and "Heartbreak Hotel, Hotel Hallelujah"—thousands come into the kingdom of God every year, as Angela's works are brought forward.

Orphanage. Today, right outside of Guatemala City, we have another example that my daughter's works follow her. There is a beautiful orphanage there that has been named after Angela. Approximately one hundred children of all ages from infancy to high school now live there.

Missions. Angela traveled and ministered in Ireland numerous times. She spent four days in Nicaragua. The pastor from Nicaragua said at her memorial service, "She's known the richest of hotels and the poorest of nations." He shared that she didn't come to Nicaragua for a vacation, but to make a deposit in the lives of the youth there. He said that today the youth of Managua, Nicaragua are on fire, doing dramas, the fruit of Angela's labors. Her works follow her.

ACCRUING OF REWARDS CONTINUES

Because our lives were so profoundly impacted by a daughter and a sister, I believe that as our family goes on to serve the Lord in our individual calls, we are bringing Angela's works forward. Similarly, because of the time and effort of my parents, especially my mother who is in heaven today, I believe that every time I obey the Lord, rewards accrue to them for the final reward time of the saints of God. My father, who is in his eighties, is still ministering as of this writing.

THE BIG WHY

I do not believe that the accruing of rewards ceases when we die. Of the great cloud of witnesses it was said, "that they without us should not be made perfect" (Hebrews 11:40). As others carry their works forward to even better and greater things, rewards continue to be accumulated to the credit of those who have died.

Chapter 11

FAITH'S GREATEST REWARD

In His third visitation, the Lord talked to me about what happens in a situation *when it appears that faith has failed*—when bad things happen to good people. It's easy to find in the Word of God not one but numerous situations where it *looked* like faith didn't work.

It appeared that faith had failed when Joseph ended up in a dungeon after he ran from Potiphar's wife, refusing to give in to her seduction. Rather than be honored and promoted by both God and man, he had an *apparent* setback and was imprisoned. Ironically, his crime was doing the right thing, the godly thing. (Genesis 39.)

It appeared that faith had failed when Daniel ended up in the lion's den. His crime was praying to God. Jealous men had plotted to remove him from his favored position as the first and preferred of the three presidents in King Darius's government. In all actuality, he was targeted "because an excellent spirit was in him" (Daniel 6:3).

It appeared that faith had failed when David, the prophesied king of Israel, ended up back in the pasture tending sheep after God used him to kill Goliath. Even worse, he ended up in the cave with four hundred distressed, indebted, and discontented men from Israel—rebels and rejects of that society—after he had been in King Saul's palace, when God used him to drive away the tormenting evil spirit. (1 Samuel 17;18; 22.)

THE BIG WHY

It appeared that faith had failed when John the Baptist's head was carried on a platter to the girl who had requested his execution. (Matthew 14:8,11.) It appeared that faith had failed when the apostle James was beheaded—at a time when the church was young and in great need of its leaders. (Acts 12:2.) And it appeared that faith had failed when Stephen's accusers "gnashed on him with their teeth" (Acts 7:54) and stoned him to death. (Acts 7:58-60.)

It certainly appeared that faith had failed as the promised Messiah, the King of kings, was hanging on a cross. Where were His royal trappings? Where were His loyal subjects? Where was all His wealth? A king? He was hanging on a cross between two thieves. His royal diadem? It was a crown of thorns. His royal vesture? He was stripped naked, with lots cast for his coat. His royal wine? It was vinegar. His adoring, cheering subjects? They were mocking spectators, spitting in His face, striking Him with the palms of their hands, crying:

> *If thou be the Son of God, come down from the cross...He saved*
> *others; himself he cannot save. If he be the King of Israel, let*
> *him now come down from the cross, and we will believe him. He*
> *trusted in God; let him deliver him now, if he will have him: for*
> *he said, I am the Son of God.*
>
> *Matthew 27:40,42-43*

But shortly after Jesus cried, "My God, my God, why hast thou forsaken me" (Matthew 27:46), His crown of thorns became a crown of glory and His cross became a throne. He pulled off the boldest, most defiant march in history, into hell itself as He took the keys to death, hell, and the grave.

FAITH HAS ITS GREATEST TRIUMPH

So where is God when the enemy goes as far as to end the life of a person? In those rare occasions where it *appears* that faith has failed, Jesus told me in His third visitation that *it didn't—faith didn't fail!* We have God's promise to recompense—even twofold, even sevenfold. We also have God's promise that the works of the departed will follow. Even more than this, the passing of God's children has actually opened the door for faith's greatest triumph. They gain heaven, which is something they cannot have in this life. We who remain on the earth have to wait until we get to heaven so we can experience it.

What the Lord said during this part of the third visitation at 6:22 A.M. was: "Most of the time, faith will overcome all of those things, but in the rare occasions when it appears that faith has failed, faith has had its greatest triumph because that person has obtained something in this life that they could not have obtained otherwise—they've obtained heaven." *In the rare occasions*—the Lord used those words. He was saying that in the exceptional, infrequent times when it *appears* that faith has come up short and someone actually dies, *faith has had its greatest triumph because that person has obtained heaven…something he or she cannot have in this life.*

I took this to mean that *most of the time* faith protects us from one of those four causes of trouble. In the rare occasions when that is not the case, if we will stay faithful, God will recompense, even double or more, and *in the earth.* Our loved ones' works will become something *even more and greater.* In addition, Christians who die get to go to heaven. Now, if they're not a Christian, that's a totally different matter. If they are, knowing that they're in heaven will strengthen us on the inside to

167

face the negative effects of the situation. The devil couldn't take away almost eighteen years of joy with Angela here and he can't take eternity away from us either.

My daughter Angela was given an eternal reward that made her happy. Faith had its greatest triumph in her life—death, hell, and the grave could not rob her of that. She wouldn't come back even if she could, and we will not look back. Satan can never threaten a Christian with dying and going to Heaven. Rewards await there and recompense awaits for those left alive. *That's why!*

Chapter 12

GRIEF, HEAVEN, AND THE
DYING PROCESS

At the Homegoing Celebration honoring my daughter Angela Nicole on January 17, 2002, my family and I addressed the crowd and thanked them for supporting us through this difficult time.

"There is a lot of sorrow," said my wife Cindy. "But since Angela did not cause us any sorrow or grief, there is no reason to let this cause us sorrow or grief in our lives."

What did Cindy mean when she said, "There is a lot of sorrow," when she then said, "There is no reason to let this cause us sorrow or grief in our lives"? There was sorrow there that day, and there was grief. There is nothing wrong with feeling either of these at certain times, on certain occasions, and to a certain degree. The loss of a child would be at the top of the list of reasons to sorrow and grieve. Even our Lord was acquainted with grief and sorrow, agony and tears. But there is a difference between being *acquainted* with something and *living* with something, even for a lifetime.

I shared with the crowd on Angela's homegoing day: "Cindy and I are so grateful for the grace of God that is upon our daughters Catherine and Jennifer, and for the power of God and place in God that is the sure and certain possession of our precious daughter Angela.

"We want you to know that there is a grace beyond the hurt. There is an anointing; there is a power in the Holy Spirit that can cover you from the depth of your soul—a place that you cannot reach with your hand, a place where you find that His grace truly is sufficient. Our sincerest desire is that this grace is yours through the power of the Holy Spirit.

"Tears can bind you, or they can set you free—and we will cry; but we will also resist sorrow like we resist sickness. A great part of our lives has been taken to heaven before us, but we will see her again—and God will wipe every tear from our eye."

RESISTING GRIEF AND ITS ADDICTION

We really don't ever know how grief will show up in someone's actions. In a way, it is like what the Lord was saying in 1 Corinthians 2:11 when He stated, "For what man knoweth the things of a man, save the spirit of man which is in him?" You see, grief is like a drug. It's addictive. Once it gets into people's emotions, there must be some kind of chemical reaction that takes place.

Most of us are somewhat familiar with what endorphins are—chemicals that are produced by our bodies and released during exercise or times of danger, pain, stress, or excitement. Endorphins cause an emotional high, a feeling of well-being, and even function as natural pain relievers. For example, when something causes pain, a nerve impulse reaches the spinal cord to release endorphins which prevent nerve cells from releasing more pain signals. Even after injury, endorphins enable humans to feel a sense of power and control over themselves that allows them to continue an activity for an extended time.

When something causes grief, there must be some kind of near-opposite chemical reaction compared to the release of endorphins, especially if grief is allowed to stay. There is no emotional high or feeling of well-being. Grief is not pain-relieving; rather, it intensifies pain that may already exist. There is no sense of power or control, but rather helplessness, hopelessness, and defeat. It shuts us down instead of giving us persistence to continue our activities in times of agony and hurt.

Grief can go deep, really deep. The problem with chemicals and addictions is that they affect the mind. The only thing that satisfies an addiction is more of the same, so when people get into grief they just get into it deeper and deeper. They can go so deep that they can't get out of it without help. As a husband and a dad, I was concerned about how my wife and daughters were going to handle their grief over Angela's passing.

The Lord spoke to me powerfully out of Isaiah 53 when He told me, "Surely I bore your griefs and carried your sorrows." (Isaiah 53:4.) He said, "If I bore your griefs and sorrows, then you're required to resist those the same way you would sickness." When Jesus gave me a revelation of Isaiah 53:4—*"Surely he hath borne our griefs..."*—it just ignited on the inside of me. That word translated "borne" is the Greek word *nasa*. This word literally means *to lift up and take off*. Living close to the NASA Space Center, I especially liked that word. Essentially what Isaiah 53:4 is saying is surely Jesus has lifted up and carried off our grief and our sorrow. That's when the Lord spoke to me to resist grief. He had given me His Word and used it to reveal the reason *why* I can resist grief.

We are able to resist sickness because with Jesus' stripes we are healed. We resist grief and sorrow the same way we resist sickness, sin, and iniquity. I had never had anybody say that to me before. When

Jesus spoke that to me, it came alive deep on the inside. God talked to me about grieving with hope—*with* hope versus *without* hope.

The Lord talked to me about resisting grief, because grief is like a spirit that can touch us deeper than our emotions. It affects our mind, but it goes beyond it, as well. It is one thing to experience sorrow, but even worse to experience grief. *Sorrow* is "distress caused by loss, affliction, or disappointment"; it is "sadness or regret." When it comes to *grief,* the dictionary defines it as "keen mental suffering or distress over affliction or loss; sharp sorrow or painful regret." Notice that grief is not just distress, but *keen mental suffering.* Grief is not just regret, but *painful regret.* It is not just sorrow, but *sharp sorrow.*

Grief hits us in a place we can't touch with our hands. It is difficult to explain. If it ever gets a hold on people, it takes them places they never want to go and holds them down much longer than they want to stay.

HEAVEN'S REALITY

What is an answer, a solution, or a cure for this grief? I must emphasize how important it was for our family to focus on Angela's gain instead of our loss. This answer—focusing on the gain instead of the loss—would not apply to every negative situation on the planet. What I offer is a key for the most extreme circumstances, such as the death of a child.

I focused on Angela's gain; this led me to desperately and intensely seek God for understanding about heaven and the kingdom of heaven itself. What the Lord told me about was the society of heaven. It became real to me that heaven is not just a place; it's a society. It is a lifestyle. It has its own mode of living, of activity.

GRIEF, HEAVEN, AND THE DYING PROCESS

God spoke this to me powerfully in my spirit: "Never say that Angela is dead." This was a major word from God that set my thinking free. He said, "Never say that Angela is dead. She's as alive today as she ever was. She just doesn't live here [on earth] anymore." That revelation exploded in me—the revelation that Angela is as alive today in heaven as she ever was on earth. She's as alive as you and me. She just doesn't live here. It's like she lives in Europe, except, instead of Europe, she lives in heaven. What is so meaningful to me is that *I know she is alive.*

I can hardly wait to see her again one day in the flesh—immortal at that. I wish I could just have a phone call with her, but it doesn't happen like that right now. I will never forget the day when I was praying to God and the heaviness was so bad. I asked Him why it felt like Angela was still right here. I even asked, "Why can't You just separate me from this feeling so the pain will leave?"

Then the Lord said to me, "It is because Angela is not dead. She's alive; she's just in heaven. She's not dead; she's alive." God healed me of that terrible pain, just like that.

When God says your child's name when He's talking to you, a million emotions go off in your spirit. God doesn't have to say your child's name or some other loved one's name for you to have the hope that they are alive. But if He does, I'm just telling you, a total awareness that they are now living in heaven will come alive in you. That's the blessed hope that every one of us can have. It will draw us to focus on the kingdom of heaven more than ever before.

Some people believe that when someone dies, their soul and spirit stay in the body here on earth, and at the Resurrection, Jesus will come back and raise the dead. In other words, until the Resurrection, they are not alive but in the grave. Some call this soul sleep.

The Big Why

But 1 Thessalonians 4:13-18 does not bear this out:

But I would not have you to be ignorant, brethren, concerning them which are asleep, that ye sorrow not, even as others which have no hope. For if we believe that Jesus died and rose again, even so them also which sleep in Jesus God will bring with him. For this we say unto you by the word of the Lord, that we which are alive and remain unto the coming of the Lord shall not prevent them which are asleep. For the Lord himself shall descend from heaven with a shout, with the voice of the archangel, and with the trump of God: and the dead in Christ shall rise first: Then we which are alive and remain shall be caught up together with them in the clouds, to meet the Lord in the air: and so shall we ever be with the Lord. Wherefore comfort one another with these words.

Paul is saying here that when the Lord returns, those who are asleep—those who are dead in Jesus Christ—will come with Him. This implies that our departed loved ones who have died in Christ are already in heaven before Jesus' return. Otherwise, Jesus could not bring them with Him at the Second Coming. Paul also says in 2 Corinthians 5:8 that to be absent from the body is to be present with the Lord.

You cannot kill the soul and the spirit of a person. That's why Moses, who had been buried fifteen hundred years before, could appear with Jesus on the Mount of Transfiguration. (Matthew 17:1-3.)

Understanding the reality of heaven—heaven is real—has helped me more than almost anything else when it came to dealing with Angela's accident. It's the overwhelming sense of finality that hurts us when we think of someone having gone to heaven. It is so common to think about what the person last said to us, the last things we did together, and the fact that they're no longer with us. That is focusing on the loss instead of the gain, and the gain is far, far greater.

Heaven is very real. It's alive. It is important to focus on the reality of what's going on there. There's a society there. I don't know if they drive cars in heaven, but they definitely get around. They travel. They visit. There are cities, trees, animals, water, and light—not necessarily sunlight as we know it here, but there is light. "And there shall be no night there; and they need no candle, neither light of the sun; for the Lord God giveth them light: and they shall reign for ever and ever" (Revelation 22:5).

It helped our family—Cindy, Catherine, Jennifer, and me—to think about the gain. Paul says, "For to me to live is Christ, and to die is gain" (Philippians 1:21). Paul is basically saying that for me to live is Christ being able to manifest Himself through me *to you* [to others], and for me to die is a gain *for me*. So he said, "I'm really torn as to which way I want to go. Do I stay or do I go?" (Philippians 1:23,24.) It is comforting to know, when we've lost a loved one, that they have gained heaven. It can be powerfully liberating.

DEATH VERSUS THE DYING PROCESS

During this time, while I was praying, the Lord spoke to me about Psalm 116:15, which says, "Precious in the sight of the LORD is the death of his saints." When we lose a loved one, there is nothing precious to us about him or her having died. It's sorrowful and grievous. It hurts; oh, it hurts. And God made us that way—to feel hurt over something painful like death.

THE BIG WHY

I was talking to God about the pain; and I was quoting that Scripture—Psalm 116:15—to Him. I asked, "God, how can it be precious to You when I'm hurting so much?"

The Lord said to me, "I didn't say the dying process is precious to me; that's the curse. What's precious to me is the death of a saint, because the death is when the spirit and soul leave the body and enter into the presence of the Lord." The step out of here into His presence—that's what is precious to the Lord.

The Lord said to me so strongly, "Death is precious to me because it's your door. But the dying process is not precious. You are to resist the dying process."

Sickness can be the dying process. Old age can be the dying process. Disease, accidents—these can be the dying process. The Lord was telling me that the dying process and death itself are two different things. Death is a door; it is a passage. We, as Christians, do not define it correctly, and we morph death and the dying process into the same entity.

Therefore, when we hear the word *death*, it affects us negatively. It evokes negative thoughts and feelings. But the word *death* quite simply means *crossing over*. The *dying process*, however, is a different matter. The last enemy that God will put underfoot will be the dying process and not death itself in the sense that death is just stepping in or crossing over. The dying process is what we still battle against today. God understands that this process is hard on us, but when the person who has died steps out of here and steps into His presence, that's the greatest victory a human being can ever experience.

POWER THINKING OR FILLING THE VOID

I want to make an important connection here in regard to the Lord's revelations to me. I want to tie these revelations to something the Lord taught me that I call "Power Thinking or Filling the Void."

In chapter 11, I discussed the subject of being transformed by the renewing of the mind. I shared that the Christian has been delivered "from the power [the control, dominion, or authority] of darkness" (Colossians 1:13). However, if he allows for darkness in his thinking, he leaves himself open and susceptible to demonic assault.

The mind is the battleground of renewal, and thoughts are the weapons of war. Thoughts have a way of growing and maturing into full-blown realities if we let them. Thoughts become opinions, which become words, which become actions...and actions can result in a quality of life that is deadly. Once a thought has jumped out of our mind and into the flesh, we create a whole new set of problems. The healthy thing to do is handle that thought in the mind before it has a chance to orchestrate our actions. We have to challenge that sinful thought on its own battlefield.

Our minds are our greatest assets (and possibly our greatest liabilities), depending on how we use them. The mind is our weapon against intellect gone-awry, vain imaginations, and negative memories. Thoughts don't have the right to be in our heads any more than a car has the right to pull into our driveway—or our garage—just because it passed down the street in front of us. We must be ready to tell intruding thoughts, "You can't stay in my life." *We* must take dominion over them—challenging our thoughts instead of our thoughts challenging us.

The Big Why

Thoughts are like visitors—they may be welcome or unwelcome. We have no control over who comes to our house and knocks on the door, but we have control over who comes in. It's the same way in the spirit. We may not have control over what we think, but we have control over what we re-think. We don't have any control over what happened in the past, but we do decide whether our past will control our present and our future.

I made a decision years ago to analyze my thoughts and refuse to let them control me. I decided to let my spirit control my thought life. It's a personal discipline. I don't like anyone engineering my thoughts. I like being renewed in the "thought reflex" of the mind or what the Bible calls the "spirit of the mind." I call it the thought reflex because everybody is affected by a wide range of things. I believe a thought can be formed based upon our sociological environment, the people we've been around, the books we've read, and the experiences we've had. A thought can be formed based upon what I'm going to call soulish DNA, because we have more than a physical DNA. We also have a mental DNA and an emotional DNA that have to be trained.

The strongholds in our minds instigate our thoughts. Strongholds are systems of thought that can lead to defeat, lifelessness, lack of joy, lack of unity, and lack of peace. *We* pull down these systematic thought patterns, ideas, and concepts and replace them with right thinking.

Entertaining the wrong kinds of memories leads to the wrong kinds of thinking in the mind of a believer. Bad memories that are entertained are door-openers for evil spirits to attack. The thoughts that we continue to dwell on from our past should not be underestimated. We have to keep our memories in check. *We* have to do this.

Grief, Heaven, and the Dying Process

As humans we tend to allow the bad experiences and memories to stand out. We allow the negatives to become a silhouette of our lives—a two-dimensional representation of an object, a dark image outlined against a lighter background. We allow the negative, dark images from our past to stand out; and we put the positives of our life in the background. This is not a full representation of our lives.

The negative past will hold us captive, dominate our conduct, and determine the outcome of our present and our future. The negative past will keep us from living in the present, let alone envisioning and planning for the future. It will rob us of vision, and the Word of God says that "where there is no vision, the people perish" (Proverbs 29:18). Parents who dwell on their negative memories will cause *bad* things to happen to themselves, their children, and the world around them. These negative memories can also prevent individuals from moving forward to bring *good* things to themselves and others.

Because of negative memories, we can end up stuck in the past or merely drifting along without purpose or momentum. Our negative experiences may have been real, but we don't have to be dominated by those memories. If we do allow them to dominate us, we can become consumed by hurt, anger, and even hate. Angela's passing was real. But my family and I chose to dwell on the good memories and on how Angela's works are following her here and now. We chose to dwell on faith's greatest reward—an eternity in the presence of God *together*. We *chose* to dwell on this.

All of us need to yield ourselves, including our thoughts, to God and what His Word says about us and our situations. It's time to celebrate our positive mileposts rather than camp out at our negative

THE BIG WHY

ones. Instead of thinking about our lives from the perspective of our negative experiences, our positive experiences should define our lives.

What I have just stated illustrates a very important point. When we renew our minds, we have to do two things. First, we must stop negative thought patterns and bring our thoughts into captivity. Secondly, we must fill the void that results with good thoughts. This is where people often miss it. If we're going to cast down an imagination, something else needs to take its place...and right away. When we cast one thing down, there's an automatic vacuum that's created that has to be filled with something else.

When we have a reason for grief or sorrow, for example, we need to think about Isaiah 53:4, where we are told that Jesus has already "borne our griefs, and carried our sorrows." We need to fill our minds with thoughts that Philippians 4:8 describes as "true...honest... just... pure...lovely...of good report." We need to focus on the gain of heaven rather than the loss of our loved one here on earth. We need to cast down the imagination of loss, and start thinking about the gain.

We can't think about the gain if we don't know about it. That's why the teachings that Jesus shared with me are so important. We need to know about the difference between death and the dying process. If we can understand the difference between the two, we can then know what to think, how to think, and probably most significant, *why we think the way we do*. This truly has been what this book is about—not just the *whys* to explain what has been unexplainable, but the *whys* to explain a new way of thinking.

We need to know what imaginations need to be cast down and how to bring our thoughts into the obedience of Christ. We also need to

180

know the thoughts to replace them. Thoughts that focus on our loved ones' gain must replace our wrong thinking; otherwise we'll have an automatic reflex and will go back to that sense of loss and resulting pain almost immediately. The fact that Jesus has *already* borne our griefs and carried our sorrows replaces our wrong thinking that we're still waiting for Him to do that. *It's already done!* We can now understand that we are supposed to resist that grief. Part of resisting is to focus on their gain instead of our loss. *The battle is in the mind.* The key to destroying the pain and hopelessness of grief is to control our thoughts, and we have to be willing to do that.

I call this "power thinking," "counter thinking," or "filling the void." We have taught people that, according to 2 Corinthians 10:5, they are to cast down imaginations and bring their thoughts captive to Christ. But the same people return to church, to the altar, to the prayer line—time and time again—with the same problems. They just don't understand that they must replace their wrong thinking with the right thinking.

Too many people are not willing to stop thinking about something that they shouldn't. They might be willing to stop talking about it, but they're not willing to stop thinking about it—because the enemy has convinced them that they are avoiding the issue, or living in denial. Somewhere along the line someone's told them, "Well, you're avoiding it." It's possible they could be avoiding the issue; but, regardless, they should start doing the right thing and rejecting their destructive thinking by casting it down and dealing with their issue in a positive, constructive manner.

This is what I determined very plainly: my daughter never gave me one day of grief in her life. Not one day. She was full of God's Spirit. She had accomplishment after accomplishment to her credit.

I thought—I *chose* to think—*I'm not going to let her home going be the horror of my life. I'm just not going to do it.* I refused to allow it to be so. The thought came first, and then I followed up the thought with how I talked and how I acted. Jesus gave me the revelation, even before I had this thought, to help me cast down wrong-thinking and have something to put in its place. The Lord helped me to understand that if I would embrace Angela's gain instead of my loss, I would get over the hurdle of grief. That's when that yoke was broken. That's when those chains fell off.

Jesus had shared with me that heaven is a society. I had these images, pictures in my mind of where Angela was and what she might be doing, to keep my thinking on track. She loved music, for example. I can actually see her singing and worshipping God in song. She loved children; and I can see her—just like my friend saw her in his dream—working with children in heaven. I can see.

In the chapters to come, I will give you some more God-thinking to replace the vain imaginations that the enemy wants to park in the garage of your mind. This thinking is about the divine ministry of comfort that the Lord provides for those who mourn. He gives us His beauty for our ashes, His oil of joy for our mourning, His garment of praise for our spirit of heaviness, and His plan of restoration to replace our desolation and waste. He gives us His plan of comfort through the Holy Spirit, through His ministering angels, and through His gift of prophecy to the New Testament church.

PART FIVE

THE
DIVINE MINISTRY
OF COMFORT

TARGETED FOR COMFORT

I used to think that comfort was simply a matter of God trying to make me feel good during a difficult time, but then I found out that comfort is very, very anointed and it has the power of the Holy Spirit in it. In the Bible, God's desire to minister divine comfort was one of the key ways that the Holy Spirit's ministry of angels was released. If we can truly take hold of this, then in our difficult times, even before our circumstances improve, we will be encouraged and know how to press toward God until we are comforted. If we seek the divine anointing in times of need, especially in stressful times, we will access the power of God on our behalf.

Isaiah 61:1-3 is a good place to begin to understand how to access the power of this divine ministry:

> *The Spirit of the Lord GOD is upon me; because the LORD hath anointed me to preach good tidings unto the meek; he hath sent me to bind up the brokenhearted, to proclaim liberty to the captives, and the opening of the prison to them that are bound; to proclaim the acceptable year of the LORD, and the day of vengeance of our God; to comfort all that mourn; to appoint unto them that mourn in Zion, to give unto them beauty for ashes, the oil of joy for mourning, the garment of praise for the spirit of heaviness; that they might be called trees of righteousness, the planting of the LORD, that he might be glorified.*

Isaiah 61:2 talks about comforting those who mourn, but then verse 3 targets a specific people to receive this comfort: "To appoint unto them that mourn in Zion." *To appoint* means to single out especially for a certain purpose. Zion, a symbol of the Christian Church today, is singled out to be the recipient of God's comfort and all that it involves. Isaiah says that the Spirit of God was upon Jesus so He could especially minister to those who are mourning in Zion—those who are hurting in the Body of Christ.

We must be careful not to use unbalanced faith teaching to conclude that just because somebody's going through a rough time, that must mean they've missed God somewhere or even sinned. No, it may just mean that this person has been attacked or is going through a trial for whatever reason. The Holy Spirit says that He especially singles out and ministers to those who "mourn in Zion."

So many people in our world today are walking around clothed in mourning! Mourning comes in different shapes and sizes, and there are different kinds and degrees. Mourning does not always have to do with the loss of a loved one. People mourn over their finances—their bank accounts or the loss of a job. They mourn over their family situations—their children or trouble with a spouse. They mourn over a loss of hope or promise, over poor decisions or lost opportunities, over past, present, and even future events, things that haven't even happened yet.

While mourning doesn't just have to do with death, we must be aware that mourning of all kinds is tied to the spirit of death. It is synonymous with grieving. There are people who feel doomed to lives of grief and despair because of their situations. They feel trapped by their circumstances. They don't think things are ever going to get better in their lives.

There is a world in mourning all around us. The use of medications to regulate emotions is at an all-time high. This is due to the pervasive heaviness and mourning in society today. These statistics should not include members of the Body of Christ.

We live in stressful times. Stress is literally killing people. Disease—the very word itself implies dis-ease. *Dis* is the Latin prefix meaning "apart or away or having a negative, depriving, or reversing effect;" and *ease* means "tranquility or rest or freedom from pain, annoyance, concern, or anxiety." Stress is ease in reverse: concern and anxiety, apart or away from tranquility or comfort. It is dis-ease; and it is a killer. People are in mourning because of this.

The Body of Christ, the Church, is supposed to be a peculiar people—not weird, but different. We are to live our lives apart from the stress and grief of life, even raised up and seated together in heavenly places in Christ Jesus (Ephesians 2:6), "far above all principality, and power, and might, and dominion, and every name that is named, not only in this world, but also in that which is to come" (Ephesians 1:21). Paul further describes this peculiar people who we as the Church, are supposed to be, when he says that God has "put all things under his [Jesus'] feet, and gave him to be the head over all things to the church, which is his body, the fullness of him that filleth all in all" (vv. 22-23).

While in this world, we are to live above its stress and mourning. Since Jesus is "the head over all things to the church" and God has "put all things under his [Jesus'] feet" then guess where Jesus' feet are? He is the head and we are His body—all things have been put under our feet. We should be living *above* the stress and grief of this world. This is where the divine ministry of comfort comes in.

The Hebrew word for "comfort" in Isaiah 61:2 is *nacham*—a very interesting word. It means "to breathe deeply, to sigh, to breathe a breath of relief." To comfort those who mourn in Zion—and the Church, as well—is to cause them to breathe a deep breath of relief.

Let's think about how it feels when there's not enough money in our bank accounts, and we're mourning because we can't pay our bills. Then the Spirit of God begins to work in our lives. Instead of fearing the end of the month, we give out a deep breath of relief—*whew*—because God provided everything we needed. We all need a divine infusion of comfort to give us beauty for ashes, the oil joy for mourning, and the garment of praise for the spirit of heaviness.

Chapter 13

COMFORT AND
BEAUTY, JOY, AND PRAISE

There is power in divine comfort—the God kind of comfort. It releases the energy of God's Spirit, the person of God that dwells in the Body of Christ today. In the earth, comfort releases the power of the Holy Spirit to work on our behalf. Isaiah 61:2 tells us that part of the role of God's Spirit is "to comfort all that mourn." Verse 3 goes on to say that God will "give unto them beauty for ashes" for those who mourn. This is part of the Holy Spirit's divine ministry of comfort—beauty for ashes.

COMFORT AND BEAUTY

According to Isaiah 61:3, those in Zion (Christians) can mourn. God's people can experience deep hurt and can have heavy hearts and minds. But they are not to stay there. Many people today are held captive by the spirit of mourning and depression. Although their futures are in front of them, they don't feel hopeful or excited. They continue to grieve and mourn over things that happened yesterday, a week ago, a month ago, a year ago, ten years ago, three marriages ago, or four children ago. Depression can be one of the strongest echoes of our pasts, and it can keep us from living beyond yesterday. I am sure that some of the people who are reading this book are all too familiar with this.

Any time we step away from yesterday and begin living for what God is doing today, old bondages like depression will come back and try to find a place in our lives. Some of us deal with depression more than others, but I think all of us have to face it at one time or another.

AN ASHES MENTALITY

Ashes are associated with mourning or, as we refer to it, with depression. Ashes are produced by something that has been burned black or charred. If we roast marshmallows and hot dogs over bright, blazing flames, we will eventually eat our fill and walk away. Pretty soon, after we stop adding fresh wood or charcoal, we will notice that the fire will die down and go out. Finally it reaches the point where it is nothing but a heap of smoldering ashes—the flame has disappeared. We can stir the ashes, but the smoldering remains will produce no more flames. Gray, charred, ash is all that remains.

Have you ever had something that was really pretty, maybe a nice sketch or drawing, and then for some reason, it was set on fire and burned up? All that was left was its ashes. Ashes represents how we feel when what we desire is destroyed or removed or is put beyond our reach. We feel so desperate, as it seems like we'll never get what we want.

Perhaps our marriage looks as if it's about to fall apart, or maybe another urgent or desperate situation is heading swiftly for the ash pile. Maybe that marriage has already fallen apart, and we're not willing to trust God for another marriage or another family...not now. We've conceded, *Well, I'll just live the rest of my life as a single person. I'm not going to do anything.*

Sometimes people have an unending list of circumstances that cause them to become burned out. Unrealized goals, dreams, ambitions, and even great calls of God have become burned to the point we no longer recognize them.

The devil has come to put his fire of hurt, adversity and mourning to the people of God. Unfortunately, many people are distorted by this kind of fire. They let it melt them, subdue them, and re-shape them into the image that the devil wants. The devil ultimately wants to reduce them to a pile of ashes so he can control them with an ashes mentality. To someone with an ashes mentality, everything appears flawed and ugly. They see no hope for tomorrow and no point to the future, and even their faces take on a dreary appearance. In today's society, *ashes* is often referred to as "burn-out."

These people are in mourning, with an ashes mentality. *Nothing* looks pretty. *Everything* looks gray. Even the color gray has a negative connotation. It is a neutral hue, with *neutral* meaning "not taking part or not aligned with or supporting any side," at a standstill, not moving. In our case, when we allow mourning to entrench in our souls, we *are* supporting a side—the side of the enemy. *Gray* is associated with dark, dismal, gloomy, dull, or dreary. These terms describe a person overcome by a spirit of heaviness quite well. They look at their spouse and think they look ugly. They look at their job—even if they're making a six-figure income—and the job looks ugly. The car they bought yesterday is suddenly a piece of junk. It may be the most beautiful day of the year outside, but they can't see it. Why? Because they're depressed. All they can see is gray.

Jesus was anointed to give you beauty for ashes. (Isaiah 61:3.) When we allow the person of the Holy Spirit to come upon us, the Spirit of God will open our eyes to the beauty around us that has been hidden from view. One of the first things we will experience is beauty in exchange for our ashes.

A DIFFERENT OUTLOOK

I've noticed that people who have just been filled with beauty for ashes are always pushing toward tomorrow—"toward the mark for the prize of the high calling of God in Christ Jesus" (Philippians 3:14). They look around them and are thankful. They see things entirely differently than the depressed person. The depressed person sees gloom in thirty-four degrees and drizzling rain, but the person who has beauty in his eyes and heart will be able to say, "Wow, this is the best duck-hunting weather I've ever seen." The husband who receives beauty for ashes comes home from work and says something nice to his wife, even when the house is a mess. When God's beauty treatment is applied to our ashes mentality, the dreary job we've held for sixteen years will turn into a blessing. We'll thank God for the steady income. In the radiance of God's beauty, the kids who appeared to be slowly eating us out of house and home will turn into blessings.

The book of Revelation tells us that God makes "all things new" (Revelation 21:5). That's what happens when we receive beauty for ashes—the burned-out part of us is exchanged for God's beauty. When we invite Jesus into our hearts and ask Him to fill us with His Holy Spirit, depression will lift. The echoes of the past will quiet down. Why? Because we are exchanging the ash heap of our depression with the beauty of God's lifestyle. When a person is bound by the spirit of mourning, his deliverance is not in Valium, a needle, or something to drink, but in declaring the promises of God to heal continually in thought and spoken word. It's a choice!

COMFORT, BEAUTY, JOY, PRAISE

Today we can be delivered from the ashes of depression and the spirit of mourning. If what we had or could have had was burned up, and all we have left is the ashes, I have some wonderful news! When the Holy Spirit's anointing comes and we allow God to begin to comfort us, out of our ashes He will give us beauty. He will give us something good where things have gone bad. A person *must* cooperate with God's techniques through correct thinking and words, to release the miracle recovery promise of "beauty for ashes."

COMFORT AND JOY

The Bible says that God will give us *joy for mourning*. The Bible says that if we'll turn our mourning over to God, His comfort will come to us. He will exchange joy for our mourning. Isaiah says that it is God's desire to appoint unto us the oil of joy. I didn't write this scripture passage; I just found out that it works. There's an oil of joy that can come from mourning. Our mourning actually becomes like a coupon that we can redeem. We present our mourning to the Lord to be paid off or exchanged with the oil of joy. There is a comfort that comes with this exchange.

It is the oil of *joy*—not heaviness and mourning—that should pervade the Church of the living God both as a whole and individually. "And the disciples were filled *with joy*, and with the Holy Ghost" (emphasis mine)—that's what Acts 13:52 tells us.

THE NECESSITY OF OIL

There is a reason that the Lord calls it the *oil* of joy. Let's consider the motor of a car. We can put gas in our engines and we can put water in our engines' radiators. Both of these are vital to the car's efficiency and life span. But gas and water will not take the place of oil. There is a price to pay if we forget to put oil in the motor or let it get really low. Oil is a lubricant. It lowers friction in the working parts of a mechanism. There are moving parts in a car motor, like pistons and rods. If the oil gets low in a motor, the motor's moving parts will start rubbing together. This produces friction which produces heat. The excess heat may weaken some of the motor's parts, causing them to bend; it may even cause some parts to weld themselves together. Sometimes the excess friction can cause the motor to simply lock up because of metal parts rubbing together so badly that they can no longer move.

LIVING MACHINES

People are like that, too. When they run out of oil in their spirits, they get into a state of mourning and their spirits become like metal grinding on metal. Life for them is grating and harsh and abrasive.

Human beings are living machines. In order to operate properly, we need more than blood coursing through our veins. There is an ingredient that runs much deeper than blood. It's called joy. Joy flows from our spirits, and it is as important to human beings as blood. While it is laughter and merriment, it is more than that. It is a rich combination of assurance, hope, anticipation, and a deep, abiding peace.

When we try to run our race in faith without joy, it's like depriving our motors of oil. Joy is the oil for our lives. Without joy in our lives, we can run for a while, but after a while things will start going wrong. Friction, overheating, and grinding will make our journey hard. It may become difficult to get out of bed in the morning. It may become a major chore to just function *period* throughout the day... every day. Our first thoughts in the morning become: *Oh, no, I have to get up today.* Instead of: *Good, Lord! It's morning!* we get up thinking, *Good Lord! It's morning again.* There's a difference between these two thoughts. The second is a far cry from, "This is the day which the LORD hath made; we will rejoice and be glad in it" (Psalm 118:24). If we don't do anything every morning except get up and comfort ourselves in God—which brings with it the oil of joy—we will release the ministry of angels. I will make this more clear in the chapter, "Comfort and the Ministry of Angels."

Incidentally, starting our day without joy makes us not worth much to ourselves, let alone to anyone else. A good illustration of this is when I was in college and had let my car run low on oil by accident. I had a nice Mercury Monterey with a slow oil leak. I didn't know about this leak because I didn't give proper attention to the upkeep of my car—I was *lacking in diligence* for this task. A friend needed my help charging the battery in his car, so I ran the jumper cable from my battery over to his. After my car ran for a little bit, my friend tried to crank his car. It just whirred and made struggling sounds.

My friend said to me, "Rev your motor up a little bit."

I did, and his car made those struggling sounds again.

He said, "Rev it up a little more."

I did, not knowing that my car was low on oil. After repeatedly revving up the engine, suddenly it sounded like I was in a war zone. My car motor exploded. It threw a rod through the motor's block, knocking a chunk out of the side. Everything on the inside seemed to crumple—being weakened by the friction and the heat—because there wasn't enough oil for proper lubrication.

A lot of people's lives are just like this. They aren't much good for themselves, let alone the people around them. One little (or big) problem, and their lives will blow up too. Without the oil of joy to be found in the Holy Spirit, they will end up locked up and even feeling blown up—devastated and in despair. Sometimes the internal friction can become so intense that people's bodies can even break down.

Isaiah said that God would comfort those that mourn and give them the oil of joy. If we can get and keep that oil on the inside, we can run our engine forever. The oil will diminish the friction and keep us from getting overheated and crumpling on the inside. It will keep things from affecting us, from rubbing us the wrong way, and from wearing us down. The joy of the Lord will be our strength. (Nehemiah 8:10.)

If we struggle with anger, we need to put down the picante and pick up the Holy Spirit, and let God give us the oil of gladness. Then when we're driving on the freeway and somebody shouts and curses at us, instead of getting all hot and bothered, we will draw from the oil of gladness. Then we can say something in our hearts like, *I'm praying for you. You're going to have to come to my church, and God's probably going to make a missionary out of you.* We won't point at this person and curse back.

COUNTERFEITS FOR JOY

The devil tries to offer counterfeits for joy. He will tempt us with all types of things such as drugs or alcohol to use to rid ourselves of the pain of depression. He may lead us into excesses in some other areas, like work or eating. These things make matters worse. After the desires of the flesh are satisfied, we will have the added problem of guilt.

The workaholic, the alcoholic, the overeater, and the drug user are all running around in circles, revving up their engines without any joy to lubricate their motors. All that the devil can ever offer is a cheap counterfeit that will ultimately leave them in bondage, causing a worse problem than they had originally. But God promises to give us the oil of joy for our mourning. One of the mightiest ministries of the Holy Spirit is to administer the oil of joy.

OIL UNDER PRESSURE

During times of pressure, I have found that the oil of the Spirit—the oil of joy—works better than at any other time. It's like making orange juice. When we squeeze the orange, instead of ruining the orange, we get orange juice. The more we squeeze, the more we get. When we receive the oil of joy while under pressure, other people see only the oil. We will radiate unexpected joy even in the midst of circumstances that would cause mourning. Whenever we're hurting, we must refuse to give in to the problems. The more pressure we experience, the more capacity we have to be joyful and rejoice in our salvation. The only way to receive the oil of joy for mourning is by prayer, good thinking, speaking faith words, and strong desire. Only the Lord can give it to us. When we receive the oil of joy for mourning, all our heated-up emotions, our depression, and our hurt will begin to subside.

In the parable of the good Samaritan in Luke 10:25-37, Jesus revealed that the good traveler used both oil and wine to help the wounded beggar he found by the roadside. This parable foreshadowed events in the Book of Acts, where the apostles and disciples of that day administered the oil and wine. In both the Old and New Testaments, oil represents the Holy Spirit. In the New Testament, wine represents the baptism of the Holy Spirit. People who received this new "wine" began to speak in other tongues and to dance and rejoice. Many who saw them thought they were drunk, but they were actually filled with new wines. What was the wine? It was the wine of the Holy Spirit. The people who had been oppressed received the oil of joy for mourning. This same wine—the oil of joy—is available today.

Accessing the Oil of Joy

Just as oil is a lubricant for a car engine, the oil of joy is the necessary lubricant for keeping our spiritual and mental engines running properly. Why do we say that joy is the lubricant of the Spirit? Because it oils our souls. The kingdom of God will come to life within us when we learn to rejoice in the God of our salvation. It will be glorious.

Paul tells us in Philippians 4:4 to "rejoice in the Lord always." When we learn to rejoice in the Lord, we may not experience joy for all things, but we can experience joy always. People who are caught up in depression, compulsive behavior patterns, and ungodly lifestyles are almost always occupied with thoughts of yesterday. A song or conversation may trigger a memory, but we must be willing to shut out the echoes.

> *Remember ye not the former things, neither consider the things of old. Behold, I will do a new thing; now it shall spring forth; shall ye not know it? I will even make a way in the wilderness, and rivers in the desert.*
>
> *Isaiah 43:18-19*

If we allow ourselves to sit around and dwell on how things used to be—whether negative or positive—the past will literally captivate our minds. It will keep us from experiencing joy today and will control our futures, because we are the sum total of what we think about and what we say. Before long, thoughts about the past will completely engulf us and choke out the newness of the life of God in us. "Therefore with joy shall ye draw water out of the wells of salvation" (Isaiah 12:3).

When Paul and Silas were thrown into jail, they decided to rejoice in the God of their salvation. (Acts 16:25.) Rejoicing in one's salvation does not just mean rejoicing over being born again. One of the meanings for the term *salvation* is "total deliverance." When we rejoice in the God of our salvation, we, too, can receive *total deliverance.*

I once heard a story about two frogs that fell into a butter churn filled with milk. At first, they just swam around. After a while, they began to tire. One frog decided to be depressed and quit—and he sank to the bottom and drowned. The other frog was determined not to go down and wouldn't give up. Pretty soon, as the milk began to thicken, he jumped onto an "island" of butter and soon jumped right out of the churn. It's the same with us. God will give us the oil of joy for mourning. We don't have to surrender to mourning since we have oil, but we do have to keep right on swimming through the challenge. Water doesn't drown us, staying under water does! Don't stay under too long. Keep kicking and keep swimming. Joy comes to you through desire, effort, self-discipline, and the wonderful promises of God.

God delivered Daniel out of the lions' den; Shadrach, Meshach, and Abednego from the fiery furnace; David, Samson, Moses, and many others from unfortunate circumstances. All these men had one thing in common: they didn't throw up their hands and quit. They kept right on swimming through their problems and received deliverance. Acts 10:34 says that God is no respecter of persons. What He has done for a multitude of others, He will do for us. It is our responsibility to not allow the devil to steal our joy. We have to keep right on swimming and the oil of joy within us—it is already within us in the Holy Spirit—will keep us from burning out. We are the lamps of this world. The only time a lamp can burn out is when it has run out of oil. God will give us the oil of joy for mourning.

We must get the oil of gladness flowing in our lives. It is part of the divine ministry of comfort that God promises in His Word. We have been appointed to receive beauty for our ashes and an oil of gladness for getting things moving again, smoothly and efficiently, and in the right direction.

COMFORT AND PRAISE

The Scripture goes on to say that God will give us "the garment of praise for the spirit of heaviness" (Isaiah 61:3). We can come to God and tell Him, "God, I've got this heaviness all over my life right now." He will say, "Bring it to Me and give it to Me. I will give you a garment of praise in its place. I will clothe you in praise." We should not be walking around wearing a garment of mourning. We should be wearing the garment of praise.

IT'S A GARMENT

I find it very significant that Isaiah doesn't just say that God will give us praise for our spirit of heaviness, but, rather the "garment" of praise. There are many kinds of garments that a person can put on, but certain garments are appropriate for certain occasions. The Bible says that God will supply a garment of praise for the spirit of heaviness. That is the right kind of garment for a depressed person to wear.

Every day I go to my closet and take out some garments that are, almost without fail, clean, fresh, and pressed. I take off my pajamas and I put on my everyday clothes—depending upon what I am going to be doing that day. My point is, the Bible says there's a garment of praise that we can put on for the spirit of heaviness. If we're going to receive the comfort of the Holy Spirit and the oil of joy for mourning, we are going to have to put on the garment of praise. One thing I know for sure, I don't care how many garments we have in our closet, none of them will put themselves on us. Some of them may have been hanging in our closet long enough that it looks like they're growing and could just walk over to us and climb on, but that isn't going to happen. We are going to have to deliberately, on purpose, put them on.

It's the same way when it comes to the things of comfort. If we have a spirit of heaviness, God isn't just going to show up and knock the heaviness out of us. He won't cause us to wake up out of this semi-quasi-foggy state of mind and emotion, praising and thanking Him for where we want to go as if we had already arrived. That's not the way it's going to happen. We're going to have to *put on* the garment of praise; we are the ones who are taking off, putting off, the spirit of heaviness. We have to initiate that exchange. The pastor can't do it for us; he cannot put on the garment of praise for us. We put on the garment of praise for the spirit of heaviness. Let's talk about how we can do this for ourselves by looking at how David put on the garment of praise.

ENCOURAGING OURSELVES IN THE LORD

David knew how to put on the garment of praise. It is called *encouraging ourselves in the Lord.* (1 Samuel 30:6.) In the Bible, David and his men found themselves in some of the worst circumstances possible. They had returned to find their city of Ziklag burned—their ashes were literal. Remember how they "lifted up their voice and wept, until they had no more power to weep" (1 Samuel 30:4)? We've already described what they saw and the loss they experienced. These mighty warriors, who would go on to perform tremendous acts of bravery, were instantly crushed in spirit. It's no wonder that they broke down and cried like little children when they returned to homes and families that were gone.

How many of us have ever wept until we literally could weep no more? Weeping is a beautiful gift of God to cleanse us on the inside, but, unfortunately, weeping does not always cleanse. Sometimes it binds us up again, depending on where we have placed our faith. Weeping can become self-focused and cause us to become more bitter than when we started. We must let weeping cleanse us instead, letting the tears remind us of the hope and cleansing we are receiving from our pains.

We must do as David did in 1 Samuel 30:6—we must encourage ourselves in the Lord, because sometimes nobody else can help us. Sometimes it is just a matter of people not knowing what to say. But David purposefully and deliberately encouraged himself in the Lord; *he* did it.

We totally miss out if we do not encourage ourselves *in the Lord,* but rather encourage ourselves in our bank account, our position at work, our talents and abilities, or our possessions. The list goes on and on. We must encourage ourselves in the Lord who does not change—who is mighty to save, whose hand is strong, who knows us by name.

We encourage ourselves by:

- Reminding ourselves of God's faithfulness in the past. This is practicing thankfulness.

- Reading the Bible to see accounts of God's numerous acts of deliverance.

- Speaking the promises of God over our lives, calling those things that are not as though they were.

- Praising God for victory and for the bright future He has in store for us.

- Challenging hurting thoughts with divine promises of healing and recovery.

- Learning how to have meaningful conversations with friends, loved ones, or associates.

- Refusing to lightly discuss serious problems.

- Rejoicing in the fact that as long as we are living, we have hope for a full recovery, restoration, and advancement.

We must encourage ourselves. We must put on the garment of praise for the spirit of heaviness.

PRAISE WILL PROTECT YOU FROM DANGER

Another powerful example of putting on the garment of praise is found in 2 Chronicles, chapter 20. Jehoshaphat was invaded by the enemy—a "great multitude" of the Moabites, the Ammonites, and others. (2 Chronicles 20:1,2.) The Bible says that Jehoshaphat and his people "feared" (v. 3). Nevertheless, they sought the Lord and encouraged themselves by *remembering* who their God was and His faithfulness in the past.

> *...If, when evil cometh upon us, as the sword, judgment, or pestilence, or famine, we stand before this house, and in thy presence, (for thy name is in this house,) and cry unto thee in our affliction, then thou wilt hear and help. And now, behold, the children of Ammon and Moab and mount Seir...how they reward us, to come to cast us out of thy possession, which thou hast given us to inherit. O our God, wilt thou not judge them? for we have no might against this great company that cometh against us; neither know we what to do: but our eyes are upon thee.*
>
> *2 Chronicles 20:9-12*

Later we see Jehoshaphat and all Judah falling before the Lord to worship Him. The priests stood up to praise God "with a loud voice on high" (vv. 18,19). They praised God "with a *loud* voice" before the victory was in sight. Jehoshaphat continued to encourage himself and his people when he told them, "Believe in the LORD your God, so shall ye be established; believe his prophets, so shall ye prosper" (v. 20).

What was God's response to Judah turning to Him and encouraging themselves in Him? The Spirit of God came upon Jahaziel, and he said,

Hearken ye, all Judah, and ye inhabitants of Jerusalem, and thou king Jehoshaphat, Thus saith the LORD unto you, Be not afraid nor dismayed by reason of this great multitude: for the battle is not yours, but God's. To morrow go ye down against them…Ye shall not need to fight in this battle: set yourselves, stand ye still, and see the salvation of the LORD with you…

2 Chronicles 20:15-17

What was the battle plan? Jehoshaphat "appointed singers unto the LORD, and that should praise the beauty of holiness, as they went out before the army, and to say, Praise the LORD; for his mercy endureth for ever" (v. 21). And what were the results?

And when they began to sing and to praise, the LORD set ambushments against the children of Ammon, Moab, and mount Seir, which were come against Judah; and they were smitten.

2 Chronicles 20:22

Talk about the power of praise! God caused the enemies to turn against each other. The Ammonites and Moabites rose against the people of Mount Seir and destroyed them; and then the Ammonites and Moabites destroyed each other. (2 Chronicles 20:23.) This important example often helps us understand why some people experience mighty recoveries and victories in life while others fail to when facing the same or similar sets of circumstances.

HABAKKUK'S SHIGIONOTH AND NEGINITH

After Habakkuk talks about vision and the robbers of vision in chapter 2, he does something very important in chapter 3. This has to do with our present discussion on comfort and praise. Habakkuk starts chapter 3 saying, "A prayer of Habakkuk the prophet upon Shigionoth" (v. 1). *Shigionoth* is a very unique word in the Bible. David uses it in the Psalms and Habakkuk uses it here. It means a song of praise, but even more, it means a song of praise that is mixed with pain. It is a song of triumph and misery at the same time. It is a song of victory and travail at the same time. While it's a song of ignorance as to *how* God's going to do it, it is a song of faith that He is *going* to do it. Habakkuk seems to say, "Man, I got this vision from God, and I know it's God; but I'm being attacked on every side." That must be how David felt in the cave of robbers at Adullam in 1 Samuel 22.

A Shigionoth is being real. It's recognizing that there is a problem and then turning to the One who can do something about it. It is praising God for victory in life, before the victory is seen. Ignoring the problem is not faith; it is living in denial. Real faith sees the problem the way it really is and then changes what exists in the natural by applying the spiritual laws of comfort. Spiritual laws are higher than natural laws. We can change outcomes within the provisions of God's promises if we will apply the laws of comfort. If we're not careful, denying or ignoring the problem can result in a failure to confront the enemy. It can result in failure to attack and defeat your difficult circumstances.

To me, the real beauty of the Shigionoth is that Habakkuk faces the pain, the misery, and the travail. He can't comprehend in the natural how a way can be made in the midst of all of this. But instead of throwing his hands up and quitting, he receives the comfort of God and begins to sing his *Shigionoth*. Habakkuk 3:17 gives us a sampling of what this is:

COMFORT, BEAUTY, JOY, PRAISE

Although the fig tree shall not blossom, neither shall fruit be in the vines; the labour of the olive shall fail, and the fields shall yield no meat; the flock shall be cut off from the fold, and there shall be no herd in the stalls.

Wow, this guy's having a bad day! It sounds as if he's lost all of his money, all of his stuff and has no ability to regain what he lost. He had a vision and now it's not happening. Who of us has ever experienced something like this? This is the "pain" part of Habakkuk's Shigionoth. However, Verse 18 has the last word. It is the praise part: "Yet I will rejoice in the LORD, I will joy in the God of my salvation."

Habakkuk says, "I have this pain going on, but I have more praise than I have pain." He says, "I'm going to Shigionoth regardless of the situation." If we would just lift our heads and our hearts and change our thoughts and words wherever we are and in whatever situation we are in and offer up a Shigionoth to God, it would be amazing what God would do for us. Habakkuk goes on to say, "The LORD God is my strength, and he will make my feet like hinds' feet, and he will make me to walk upon mine high places. To the chief singer on my stringed instruments" (v. 19).

That's Habakkuk's song. Like the little ole deer that can outrun the enemy, we, too, can be put in the right place—in "high places." That's where our high praises are.

Habakkuk is saying, "Give me that guitar. Give me that piano. Give me that CD or DVD player. Give me that radio. That's my stringed instrument." The Hebrew word for stringed instrument is a beautiful word. It's an interesting word, as well—*neginoth*. It means an instrument that we use to praise God with our Shigionoth.

THE BIG WHY

Habakkuk is saying, "This negative circumstance has to change! I'm going to take my neginoth and give God some Shigionoth. I'm not going to take Metallica and phase back into yesterday, and sing and play songs like 'All Nightmare Long' or 'Harvester of Sorrow.' I'm not listening to Tupac on my neginoth, playing and singing 'So Many Tears' or 'Temptations' or 'God Bless the Dead.' I'm not listening to Country Western music on my neginoth, with its 'He Stole My Woman' and 'She Stole My Man' songs. When I get into my car, I turn my neginoth on and it better be putting out some Shigionoth to God; or I will go to another station."

Paul and Silas were in jail at midnight and they began to offer a Shigionoth to God. They began to sing praises, and the supernatural power of God comforted them and literally broke open the prison.

> *And at midnight Paul and Silas prayed, and sang praises unto God: and the prisoners heard them. And suddenly there was a great earthquake, so that the foundations of the prison were shaken: and immediately all the doors were opened, and every one's bands were loosed.*
>
> *Acts 16:25-26*

Paul had been thrown into prison for his Christian teachings. He had done nothing wrong, but he was in prison. It seemed like faith had failed. Silas, who traveled with him on his evangelistic trip, was imprisoned with him. Can we picture them in jail? Whipped and thrown into the lower prison, with their hands and feet placed in painful stocks. Who knows what thoughts of depression they had to fight off—but they did it. Even in the depths of a Roman jail, these two great men of God found a reason and a way to praise God. Paul and Silas weren't happy about being in jail, but they chose to put on the garment of praise instead of the spirit of heaviness. Your situation may have not brought you to a literal prison, but it can have you feeling just as imprisoned in your family, finances, happiness, your job, or some other very important part of your life.

When we praise God, He will bring us divine comfort.

The Shigionoth says, "Things haven't changed yet, not all the way, but in here, in my spirit, I know they're going to change. So, I'm just going to give You the praise anyway, God." God in return says, "I will make an exchange with you. I will give you the oil of gladness for your mourning, the garment of praise for your spirit of heaviness." (Isaiah 61:3.) Things don't have to have changed yet on the outside, but if they change on the inside of us, they're going to change on the outside of us, too. That's one of the divine powers of the Holy Spirit.

We must pay close attention to this: Father God, Jesus, and the Holy Spirit never said that we're going to have everything taken care of and corrected up front before we ever face it. What God did say, however, was, "I'm going to be with you. I'm going to go with you. If your adversary tries to stop your vision, your plan, your call, your purpose or anything else, if you will just think the right thoughts, talk the right talk, walk the right walk, and let the comfort of God come in, the enemy will not win." (Matthew 5:3-12.)

Jesus is telling us today what He told the woman with the issue of blood in Mark 5—you're whole beginning right now. (Mark 5:34.) In the Greek, there are two different words for "whole" here—one has a present inference and the other has a future and ongoing inference. Just one English word in our translations, yet there are two words that Jesus actually spoke. In essence, He said, "Your faith has brought healing to you; but if you'll receive this comfort now, you'll start recovering from everything." She fell down at His feet and gave Him a Shigionoth. If we need some of the divine comfort that releases the power of the Holy Spirit, then it is time to lift our hearts and voices and give God a Shigionoth—praise that comes from the assurance of God's comfort that in turn releases God's power. That is one way that comfort can come in a stressful time.

COMFORT AND CONFESSION

It is difficult to separate praise from confession, so I will include in our discussion of praise the power of confession to access the divine ministry of comfort. When Jesus looked at the woman with the issue of blood He said, "Daughter, be of good comfort" (Matthew 9:22). We must be ready to rejoice in every circumstance. Don't back off. Keep flowing and going forward. Let our mountain hear our voice. Jesus says, "That whosoever shall say unto this mountain, Be thou removed" (Mark 11:23). He didn't say that our mountain needs to hear our pastor's voice but that it needs to hear *our* voice.

Encouraging ourselves in the Lord—a form of praise—puts our focus on the goodness and faithfulness of God. We start thinking about right things—things that are true. Remember "For as he [a man] thinketh in his heart, so is he" (Proverbs 23:7). Our destiny is connected to the thoughts that we think in our hearts.

Our hearts control our speech. One of the best ways to find out if we are thinking correctly is by what we say. Luke 6:45 tells us, "A good man out of the good treasure of his heart bringeth forth that which is good; and an evil man out of the evil treasure of his heart bringeth forth that which is evil: for of the abundance of the heart his mouth speaketh."

The Bible tells us that with our words we can oftentimes create our reality: "A man's belly shall be satisfied with the fruit of his mouth and with the increase of his lips shall he be filled. Death and life are in the power of the tongue: and they that love it shall eat the fruit thereof" (Proverbs 18:20-21). In other words, what we choose to say is what we will have. We can, "[call] those things which be not as though they were" (Romans 4:17). Thinking the right things leads to saying the right things. Thinking about God's plan for our lives brings comfort. Speaking those things reinforces those comforting thoughts, and the next thing we know, we are experiencing comfort instead of ashes, mourning, and heaviness. True power-releasing comfort—the divine kind of comfort—will have its basis in God and His Word.

Proverbs 4:20-22 says something very supportive of this: "My son, attend to my words; incline thine ear unto my sayings. Let them not depart from thine eyes; keep them in the midst of thine heart. For they are life unto those that find them, and health to all their flesh." The Word of God that we have before our eyes until it goes into our hearts will be health to our flesh. How do we know that God's Word is in our hearts? It will come out of our mouths. We will say God's Word instead of the circumstances. We will say what God says about our situations rather than what our past says. We will say what God says about our situations rather than what society, the economy, or the government says.

The Bible says, "Put me in remembrance: let us plead together: declare thou, that thou mayest be justified" (Isaiah 43:26). What does that mean? It means that we can remind God of what His Word says and of what He has done in the lives of men and women throughout history. What He has done for Moses, Abraham, Solomon, Paul, and many others, He will also do for us.

When we begin to praise God and repeat His Word back to Him, the spirit of heaviness will lift. As new things start happening, we should continue to stay close to the Word of God—no matter what happens, good or bad. If we're sad, we rejoice; if we're hurting, we rejoice. If we don't have enough money in the bank, we rejoice. At all times we should thank the Lord that He supplies all our need "according to his riches in glory by Christ Jesus" (Philippians 4:19). Even when things are going well, we rejoice so we can build up our praise for when we need it later. There's no such thing in the Scripture as comfort without confession. Confession is actually a form of praise. Praise is the act of expressing approval or admiration in words or song, and there is no higher praise than to quote and live by someone's words. There is hardly anything that makes a parent feel more appreciated than when their children repeat what they have said as being what they, too, believe and aspire to live by.

In Isaiah 61, when the Scripture says that it's God's plan "to comfort all that mourn" (v. 2), the following verse makes reference to "the garment of praise." Praise is a part of God's plan for comfort. It is clear that when people have divine comfort, they begin to say and do a higher thing than they did before. Knowing God's promise of comfort will evoke praise to release comfort; once that comfort is released, it will result in more praise and confession, which just keeps the comfort coming.

Chapter 14

COMFORT AND RESTORATION

We're still on the subject of the power of divine comfort. We have looked at Isaiah 61:1-3, and that was powerful enough. But there is more. *Recompense* and *restore* are nearly synonymous in meaning. This teaching on restoration will further enhance what was already revealed about recompense.

The Bible says that part of the ministry of the Holy Spirit is "to comfort" (Isaiah 61:2). It goes on in verse 4 to include restoration as part of this package: "And they shall build the old wastes, they shall raise up the former desolations, and they shall repair the waste cities, the desolations of many generations." Just as surely as God promises the Holy Spirit Himself, He promises His anointing for restoration.

Isaiah said that it was the Spirit of the Lord God—"The Spirit of the Lord God is upon me; because the Lord hath anointed me" (Isaiah 61:1)—that was empowering this assignment. Just as the Lord came to give us beauty for ashes, the oil of joy for mourning, and the garment of praise for the spirit of heaviness, He came to give us restoration in the place of our desolation and waste.

This anointing of restoration is for cities...for nations...for generations. God knows how to get generations back to us. I have confessed and I have prayed that in my lifetime everything the Hallam, the White, and the Bradley families lost in the twentieth century will be returned. The Whites and Bradleys are the other sides of my family.

THE BIG WHY

I'm calling for this restoration in my family in the twenty-first century according to the promise of Isaiah 61:4. It has and will continue to be my prayer and declaration.

Along this line, God and His plan for our lives have been sorely misunderstood. In what could be the last days here on planet Earth, much of the end-time theology of the church is focused on chaotic, judgmental happenings. Surely God is very much into rooting out, pulling down, destroying, and throwing down things that are contrary to His plan. Unfortunately, this has all been lumped into one category called *judgment*—and that is not an accurate picture of what is actually going on.

God's aim is to get us right so we can experience His best for us. He is not a God of destruction, *but of restoration*—of renewing hope, vision, and strength. Even in the Old Testament writings, Isaiah's message is broken into three parts: thirty-nine chapters deal with judgment, sixteen chapters deal with comfort, and the remaining eleven deal with hope. Isaiah's main message—and God's main message—is one of salvation. God is not interested in sin-management any more than He's interested in correction. They are means to an end, but not the end in itself. God is about life, and life in abundance. There is *life* at the end of the tunnel!

To get us to this place, sometimes God may yell—just like we would if our child was about to run out into the road in front of a tractor trailer. Unfortunately, when God raises His voice, there are those who are quick to say that this can't be love—that love does not raise its voice. What a foolish conclusion! God might rebuke us (pointing out the reality of a situation), but His greater joy is refreshing us. He will convict us, but His greater thrill is to inspire encouragement, hope, *and comfort*, including restoration.

COMFORT AND RESTORATION

Especially in the past, some people have mistakenly been so spiritual minded that they have crippled their opportunity to be of earthly good. Some people don't even enjoy their earthly journey, and have no hope of seeing anything restored in their lives. They have been blinded to God actually being concerned about life on this earth. The Bible says that God wants our lives to be good "on earth *as it is in heaven*" (Matthew 6:10, emphasis mine). God made provision for this to happen. The divine ministry of comfort through the power of the Holy Spirit is part of that provision. That ministry includes restoration.

God does not build on a foundation of sand or sin. His first focus may have been rooting out wrong things, pulling down things that are tainted or corrupt, and destroying things that are not of Him. But to build, to raise up, to repair—not to destroy—is His primary and ultimate goal. "And they shall *build* the old wastes, they shall *raise up* the former desolations, and they shall *repair* the waste cities, the desolations of many generations" (Isaiah 61:4, emphasis mine).

I believe that as we become more conformed to the image of our dreams and desires, we will see more things restored. We will look at people and situations, and instead of seeing and settling for hopelessness, we will see the potential for a miracle and for restoration. I believe that we will go a step further. I believe that it is our right to expect and declare restoration in this hour, and so we will. When we do this, we are not demanding anything of God—we are not ordering God to do anything. We are simply taking hold of what God has already provided. I like what Isaiah 42:22 says in this regard: "But this is a people robbed and spoiled; they are all of them snared in holes, and they are hid in prison houses: they are for a prey, and none delivereth; for a spoil, and none saith, Restore."

THE BIG WHY

This certainly is a picture of what happens to people who are caught up in grief and mourning in today's world. "And none saith, Restore." Well, I, for one, will not remain silent. I say, *"Restore!"* I call for a restoration of what "the locust hath eaten, the cankerworm, and the caterpillar, and the palmerworm" (Joel 2:25). I choose to join the ranks of Isaiah 58:12: "And they that shall be of thee shall build the old waste places: thou shalt raise up the foundations of many generations; and thou shalt be called, The repairer of the breach, The restorer of paths to dwell in." A very plain rendering of this statement is found in the *Message Bible:* "You'll use the old rubble of past lives to build anew, rebuild the foundations from out of your past. You'll be known as those who can fix anything, restore old ruins, rebuild and renovate, make the community livable again."

"For your shame ye shall have double; and for confusion they shall rejoice in their portion: therefore in their land they shall possess the double: everlasting joy shall be unto them" (Isaiah 61:7). Everywhere our problems have tried to put us down, God is going to jump into our circumstances and give us double. He said He will give us double—double what the curse tried to take from us. Maybe years ago someone used to smoke really badly and God finally set him free, but he's still having a problem in his lungs. He ought to grab this verse and begin to say, "Everywhere my past failings have tried to attack me, hurt me, shame me, claim me, put me down, torment me, I'm calling for double... including healing in both lungs."

Someone may say, "Well, Pastor, you keep preaching prosperity to these folks, but it hasn't worked for me. I've already lost a million dollars."

For your shame, God will give you double. Hear me: your first million is not your last million. So what if you've lost your first million;

start working on your next one. Work on it in faith. I've heard people dwelling on and saying that kind of silly, negative stuff. Let's not go around saying that. Let's get to work, expecting God's "double."

"Therefore in their land *they shall possess* the double" (v. 7, emphasis mine). God says He is going to give it to us, but *we have to possess it…* lay hold of it. Remember that faith has a voice. We must speak the right things and not the silly stuff.

Praise God for the ministry of comfort that not only promises beauty for ashes, the oil of joy for mourning, and the garment of praise for the spirit of heaviness…but restoration for our desolation.

Chapter 15

JESUS' MINISTRY OF COMFORT

I started my study of the divine ministry of comfort in Isaiah, chapter 61. Isaiah 61:1-3 was the same Scripture reference that Jesus used for His first public message recorded in Luke 4:18-21. In this passage in Isaiah, Isaiah prophetically stated that the Spirit of the Lord was upon Jesus to comfort those who mourn in Zion. When Jesus stood in the temple, He took the scrolls of Isaiah, opened them, and began to read:

> *The Spirit of the Lord is upon me, because he hath anointed*
> *me to preach the gospel to the poor; he hath sent me to heal*
> *the brokenhearted, to preach deliverance to the captives, and*
> *recovering of sight to the blind, to set at liberty them that are*
> *bruised.*
>
> *Luke 4:18*

This was Jesus' first message, and I believe that He read that passage over and over when He preached it everywhere He went. I don't believe He preached it just that one time in the temple, but that everywhere He went He declared: "The Spirit of God is upon Me. He has anointed Me to do some things."

Then Jesus would speak about what His Father could and would do. He proclaimed, "God will comfort those who mourn." Jesus' ministry was one of comfort. For example, in the Sermon on the Mount in Matthew 5, He taught, "Blessed are they that mourn: for they shall be comforted" (v. 4). But Jesus had much, much more to say than this when it came to comforting His people.

THARSEO—COURAGE AND BOLDNESS FOR BATTLE

The Greek word for *comfort* in Matthew 9:22 is *tharseo;* and it literally means "courage or boldness." It refers to the kind of comfort or encouragement that troops need before going into battle. Imagine a commander, an army general, knowing that his troops are about to go into a very intense battle, and knowing that they can win if they'll not lose their nerve. So he gets before them and he starts talking to them. He reminds them of how they've been trained—how they've gone through boot camp and special military operations, how they have the necessary equipment, artillery, camaraderie, and battle plan. He tells them, "We can win this battle and we're going to!" Something happens to these troops; their courage begins to rise up inside. They have received comfort—*tharseo*—encouragement before going into battle.

Since I had experienced supernatural comfort in my own life, I wanted to know more about it. My search led me to Matthew 9, where I found the story of the woman with the issue of blood.

And, behold, a woman, which was diseased with an issue of blood twelve years, came behind him [Jesus], and touched the hem of his garment: for she said within herself, If I may but touch his garment, I shall be whole.

But Jesus turned him about, and when he saw her, he said, Daughter, be of good comfort; thy faith hath made thee whole. And the woman was made whole from that hour.

Matthew 9:20-22

From that moment, from that hour, the woman became progressively better. The woman who had been sick was made whole after twelve years of mourning, after twelve years of problems—physical, financial, social...in every way. What an illustration of faith! God said in Isaiah 61 that through the ministry of Jesus and His Spirit, He would comfort those that mourn. It is significant that Jesus used Isaiah 61 for His first public message recorded in Luke 4:18. God wants comfort to come into our lives when and where we need it, but we have to receive it.

The woman in Matthew 9 came to Jesus and touched the hem of His garment. Both Mark and Luke say that she knew immediately that she was made whole. (Mark 5:29; Luke 8:44.) However, she hadn't gotten her money back, *not yet*, where she "had spent all her living upon physicians" (Luke 8:43). She hadn't gotten all of her strength back, *not yet*. She still had some physical recovery up ahead from the effects of twelve years of pain. Though "straightway the fountain of her blood was dried up, and she felt in her body that she was healed of that plague" (Mark 5:29), *there was still a battle ahead.*

The woman—in response to Jesus' question in Luke 8:45, "Who touched me?"—fell down before Him and told Him why she had touched Him. She had said to herself that if she could just touch His garment, she would be made whole, though she didn't know *how* that was going to happen. Jesus responded by saying, "Daughter, be of good comfort: thy faith hath made thee whole; go in peace" (Luke 8:48).

What Jesus said in essence to her was, "Woman, I have good news for you. When you touched the hem of My garment and said within yourself, *When I touch Jesus, I'm going to be whole,* the power of God began to work for you. What you believed for, happened. Now, get ready. You *have* received, and *are going* to receive. What you received, you're going to have to maintain. Your total recovery *is beginning* this very hour. If tomorrow the symptoms try to come back and it looks like you don't have everything back *yet*, just keep praising God. Keep doing what you did when you fell down here before Me just a moment ago, because from this hour, this is how it works. You're going to get better and better and better and better and better."

It was crucial that the woman with the issue of blood receive the comfort that Jesus had to give, because her getting better was going to depend upon that divine comfort to keep the miracle power of God flowing. It was going to be very important for the oil of joy that comes with divine comfort, to continue to protect her faith in the days to come. I belive that is one of the reasons why some people keep their healing and others fail to—the *why* of comfort.

I have some wonderful news! When we allow the comfort of God to come into our lives, we have it now and we'll get better beginning right now. But there is an exchange involved here. Perhaps we don't have the money that we need *yet*. We tell Jesus, "You told me that I was going to be whole, but I still have some bills out there. I'm trying the best I can, but it just looks like I have more bills than I have money. But, God, You're the one who supplies all of my need. You said that You would, so I'm going to give You the praise right now in advance."

That's the exchange. We give Him our problems, our mourning, our ashes, and in exchange He gives us comfort, beauty, joy, and the garment of praise. That's exactly what the word *tharseo* means—courage and boldness, encouragement and comfort even before the battle.

PARAKLEETOS—TO BE WITH US

In John, chapter 14, two separate verses—verses 16 and 18—have two totally different words in the Greek to reference *comfort*. God anoints the Holy Spirit with both, because God knows the need that we have for comfort—not pity or sympathy—but comfort. God takes our mourning personally and tells us He will comfort us.

Jesus says in John 14:15-16: "If ye love me, keep my commandments. And I will pray the Father, and he shall give you another Comforter, that he may abide with you for ever." The Greek word for "Comforter" here is the word *parakleetos*. We can find this word quite often in the Scriptures where we see references to works of the Holy Spirit. It's a word for "helper" or "the one who is with us or stands by us or goes with us." *Parakleetos* actually means "to come along and assist, to support, to be with us." The Bible says in Romans 8:26, "Likewise the Spirit also helpeth our infirmities: for we know not what we should pray for as we ought: but the Spirit itself maketh intercession for us with groanings which cannot be uttered." The Holy Spirit is our helper. He comes in there and assists. He gets hold of the situation with us. One Bible translation says that He comes alongside.

Jesus says, "And I will pray the Father, and he shall give you another Comforter, that he may abide with you for ever" (John 14:16). Since Jesus prayed for "another" Comforter, that must mean that Jesus Himself is a Comforter. When He says that God is going to give us *another* Comforter, "even the Spirit of truth" (v. 17), He is referring to the Holy Spirit. He will come alongside and assist us, support us, and be with us. He will give us physical, emotional, and spiritual support. He is a companion who is with us at all times—"that he may abide with you for ever" (v. 16). Jesus said, "I will not leave you comfortless" (v. 18). He will "bring all things to your remembrance, whatsoever I [Jesus] have said unto you" (v. 26)—the right words at the right time. Now that's a helper!

Oftentimes Cindy and I will start talking about something, and I'll forget a word or someone's name. I'll say, "Oh, what's their name?"

Cindy will answer, "So-and-so."

Then I'll say, "Yeah, that's the name! Thank you, honey." And we'll keep on talking. Cindy is helping me when she does that. It's the same with the Spirit of God. He will help us remember things, things we need to know. He helps us. He helps our prayer life. He's a comforter. There is something about knowing that the Lord is beside us that brings great comfort. Then we can just breathe a big sigh of relief—*whew!*

Earlier in the book, I shared the story of when I drowned at youth camp when I was eight. For the next couple of years the experience traumatized me. I had a morbid fear of getting into water that was over my chest. My pride had caused me to foolishly jump into the lake at youth camp, and now my pride was really bothering me. I had all the necessary skills for swimming in deep water, but I didn't have the peace and assurance to do it. So my daddy, with his Marine Corps background and not-backing-down attitude, finally said, "Now, Son, you are going to have to learn to swim. You are going to have to break this fear."

He had me step out onto the diving board of a little pool. He got into the water and stood around eight to ten feet away from me. Then he said "Okay, I want you to jump. Just like you glide in the shallow part, you jump in and glide right here; and Daddy's going to go with you. I'll go right with you."

I said, "Daddy, I can't do it."

He said, "Oh, yeah! Yeah, you can! You can do it! Nothing's going to happen to you. I'm right here." I knew he meant business when he called me Walter Glenn. He said, "Now, Walter Glenn, I'm standing right here. And look! I can almost reach you; you're going to be fine. Just jump off and swim over here to me. Just like you do over in the shallow side, do the same thing right here. Daddy's going to be right here; you're going to be fine."

I said, "No, I ain't going to do it!" I said, "I can't do it!"

Finally he got tired of all that. If it had been one of my sisters that he was working with, he would have said, "That's okay, sweetie. You just go on over there and sit down." But this was one of his boys. So he said, "I'm going to count to three, son; and if you don't jump off of that board and swim to me..." You need to understand that this was after about a half hour of his trying to get me to jump in, and he was already turning into a prune standing in the water. He said, "If you don't jump off that board, I'm going to come get you and throw you in."

"One...," Daddy started counting.

"Daddy, I don't want to do it," I yelled.

"Two..."

"I don't want to do it."

"Here I come...*three.*"

Zoom! I jumped off the board because my fear of my daddy was greater than my fear of the water. I jumped into the pool, and when I got beside Daddy, he just swam right along with me all the way to the other end. I swam so hard that I bumped my head on the other end of the pool. After that, I never had another day of problems with swimming because Daddy went right beside me the whole way.

That's exactly what the word *parakleetos* means. Jesus said that He would pray to the Father to send another Comforter who would go with us. We can risk it because the Holy Spirit is going to be with us all the way. You see, the Holy Spirit is not a mere religious figment of our imaginations. It is *He*, the Spirit of Truth. It is *He*, the Comforter, but we have to let Him do His work. What He won't do—like my dad threatened to do—is grab us and throw us into the pool. We have to do that part ourselves, but He will be there with us all the way—"for ever" (John 14:16).

I went into the delivery room with Cindy when all three of our daughters were born. I don't mind telling mothers that I have enormous respect for them. I hear guys talk about how they went into the delivery room with their wives, like it was some big thing on their part. My response is: "Don't brag to me, man; I know what goes on in there—*and it's all about the woman*. All you are is a spectator."

Both of us had gone through Lamaze classes where we learned to pant and puff and all that kind of stuff. I think it worked, though I'm not sure. At least it made us *think* something good was happening. So I went in there with Cindy when she was going to have the baby. I was holding her little hand, and there we were. You have to know that my wife is so cool; she is so well-spoken and calm. I'm one of the most blessed husbands who ever lived. You just don't know how blessed I am.

When Cindy had our three children, she had them with her eyes wide open, and she refused to scream. She was just gritting her teeth. I wanted to say, "You want a piece of rawhide or what?" I mean, as a husband, what can you do—get her a stick to chew on?

She was determined: "No, I'm going to do this." And she did. Pretty cool thing.

While it was happening, I stood beside Cindy as long as I could. I held her hand and kind of stroked her hair. I talked with her, because she was going through all this stuff that only ladies really know about. However, while I was standing there, I was thinking, *My God! I'm the one in near-shock here. I'm the one who needs oxygen in this place. And* I'm *supposed to be comforting* her! Nevertheless, I continued to comfort Cindy the best that I knew how.

That's what the Holy Spirit does for us—*though He does it much better.* Jesus said that He would pray to the Father to send another Comforter who would go with us all the way. And the Father did just that. That is why some people make it all the way through to the other side of physical pain, or financial, emotional, or family stress. The Spirit of Comfort goes all the way!

ARPHANOS—NO ORPHANS

Then in John 14:18, Jesus says, "I will not leave you comfortless: I will come to you." Here He uses a totally different word for comfort. This is the Greek word *arphanos.* We get the word orphan from this word.

Jesus has already told us that He is the *parakleetos*—that He is not going to make us go through life by ourselves. Then He says that He will not leave us *an orphan.*

THE BIG WHY

In the day that Jesus spoke these words, orphans were in very dire straits, in extremely sad and difficult situations, because they were pretty much on their own. The orphanage outside of Antigua, Guatemala, named in honor of Angela by my dear brother Ivan Tait, cares for nearly one hundred children. If it weren't for the orphanage, they all would have died very young, almost without exception.

Jesus says in John 14 that He will not leave us without a parent. He says that He will be our parent. That's a beautiful thought! Jesus is saying that we'll not be left feeling like we don't have a mother or a father, like we're abandoned, like we don't know our heritage, or what to expect in life. Anyone who has been orphaned in life knows exactly what I'm talking about.

If we grow up not knowing our mother and father or where came from, then we might have some questions about where we're going. We might wonder what we're going to look like since we don't know our parents and their physical traits. We might have some questions about how we're going to turn out, since we don't know what other things we might have inherited from our parents, like personality traits, talents, or natural tendencies for certain things.

Jesus is in essence saying, "Listen, I'm not going to leave you that way. I'm going to be with you. You're going to know where you came from. You're going to know Who's with you. You're going to know where you're going. You're going to know who you are *because you're going to know Whose you are.*"

I get excited thinking about this. May God help us as the Body of Christ today, to not have an identity crisis, but to know who we are. Why is it okay for the Muslims to be loud and bold and to pray on airplanes and challenge the courts? Why is it that the world wants to agree to abortions and things like it, while Christians shut up and act like they don't know who they are? Some Christians think they have to act like the world to be a witness—they think that's what Paul meant when he said, "I am made all things to all men, that I might by all means save some" (1 Corinthians 9:22)—or else they *are* like the world. For further clarification on what Paul meant, it helps to read this passage in context:

> *For though I be free from all men, yet have I made myself servant unto all, that I might gain the more. And unto the Jews I became as a Jew, that I might gain the Jews; to them that are under the law, as under the law, that I might gain them that are under the law; To them that are without law, as without law, (being not without law to God, but under the law to Christ,) that I might gain them that are without law. To the weak became I as weak, that I might gain the weak: I am made all things to all men, that I might by all means save some. And this I do for the gospel's sake, that I might be partaker thereof with you.*
>
> *1 Corinthians 9:19-23*

We need to know who we are. One thing's for sure: we are not orphans. We have the spirit of righteousness, holiness, godliness, and joy—even in difficult times. Jesus says He will comfort us and will not leave us without identity.

I generally don't know how people started out in life. I can understand if they struggle with identity problems in the natural. I can pray and believe that they will get their answers about who they are, but it's the higher answer that matters most—who they are in Christ.

Peter the disciple didn't know who he was. One time Jesus asked him and the rest of the disciples, "Whom do men say that I the Son of man am?" (Matthew 16:13).

The disciples answered, "Some say that thou art John the Baptist: some, Elias; and others, Jeremias, or one of the prophets" (v. 14).

Then Jesus asked, "But whom say ye that I am?" (v. 15).

Peter answered, "Thou art the Christ, the Son of the living God" (v. 16).

And Jesus said to Peter, "Blessed art thou, Simon Bar-jona: for flesh and blood hath not revealed it unto thee, but my Father which is in heaven...Thou art Peter, and upon this rock I will build my church; and the gates of hell shall not prevail against it" (v. 17,18).

Peter had been called Simon Bar-jona up until that time, but when he found out for sure who Jesus was, Jesus just stopped and said, "Now I'm going to tell you who *you* really are."

I'll make this clear: the moment that we identify with Jesus is the moment we find *our* identity. That is when we begin to realize who we really are: "[We] are a chosen generation, a royal priesthood, an holy nation, a peculiar people; that [we] should shew forth the praises of him who hath called [us] out of darkness into his marvelous light" (1 Peter 2:9). The time came when Peter said, "We *were* not a people, but today *we are* the people of God." I get excited when I think about this.

We don't have to bounce around aimlessly throughout our lives, not knowing who we truly are and why we were created. When I was a little boy, my daddy used to say, "Son, if you don't stand for something you'll fall for anything." *We have to know who we are.* Your identity determines your destiny! You may not like how you began in life, but you can change your future, if you know who you are. Are we getting the message? *We have to know who we are.* My parents used to say to me, "Now, you're *our* son. We don't care what anybody else is doing; you're *our* son."

I'd say, "But, Daddy, everybody else is doing it. Why can't I?" Have you ever heard that line before?

My daddy would respond, "Oh, no, *everybody* else isn't doing it. Everybody else isn't doing it because *you're* not. I don't care how much *they* party, how much *they* sin, how much *they* do this or do that— *you're* not doing it. So that means that *not everybody* is doing it." These activities were not my parents' idea of a proper lifestyle, in light of who they were and what they believed. These activities and behavior were not part of the identity I had through my parents. Therefore, I continued to identify with my strengths instead of my weaknesses.

I'll never forget when I was in the ninth grade, and I was in love with this girl. I knew it was real because, after all, it was the ninth grade. Any parents who allow their son or daughter to date in the ninth grade need reconsider that position. It's all right if people disagree with me over this. Parents will get over it after a while, after they have have walked their teens through all the counseling sessions, broken hearts, and worse conditions that generally follow the actions of young teens today out on dates by themselves.

Here's the situation: my parents wouldn't let me date in the ninth grade. Today I thank God for that, because in the ninth grade I was dealing with lust and hormones. But at that time, I said, "Daddy, I really like this girl."

He said, "Well, son, I don't mind you liking that girl, you just can't get hooked up with that girl. I mean, you can like her, but you're not going to be dating, and you're not going to have *one* girlfriend. It just isn't going to happen in the ninth grade. Forget it! You can like all the girls in the school, but you can't like just one—because if you like just one, I'm going to get involved."

I'm thinking, *Oh, Lord! Don't let my daddy get involved, whatever You do.* I remember saying this to him, "Well, Daddy," and I was all upset, "you're just not trying to get along with me." I thought I was making a very good point, and that I had gotten to him.

Daddy replied, "Son, I'm not raising you to get along *with me*. I'm raising you to get along *without me*."

Does that ever make sense to me today. It didn't make any sense to me back then, but it makes all the sense in the world today. Oh, the worth of having identity! Jesus says that He will not leave us without identity. We will not be an *arphanos*. Our identities are shaped just as much by God and His family as they are with our families here on earth. You can change your messes into successes if you know who you are. We are not orphans.

Chapter 16

COMFORT AND
THE NEW TESTAMENT CHURCH

The divine ministry of comfort is powerful. It's throughout the Old and the New Testaments. We've read about it in the Old Testament and in the life of Jesus in the New Testament. We can also see this ministry continued through the apostle Paul for the Church. Jesus' ministry was a ministry of comfort—the Apostle Paul deals with this ministry in the Bible on yet another level.

SOMPARAKALEO—TO COMFORT JOINTLY

Keep in mind that the ministry of Jesus, according to Isaiah 61:2 and 3, was designated to comfort those who mourn in Zion—which also refers to *the church today*. Notice what Paul writes in Romans 1:10-12:

> *Making request, if by any means now at length I might have a prosperous journey by the will of God to come unto you. For I long to see you, that I may impart unto you some spiritual gift, to the end ye may be established; that is, that I may be comforted together with you by the mutual faith both of you and me.*

Paul writes to the church at Rome, telling them that he is asking God to give him a prosperous trip. He tells them that he can hardly wait to see them because he wants to impart a spiritual gift to them—an anointing. He says they will be strengthened and established by this gift, and then both parties will be blessed as the faith they have in common will be *comforting* to both of them.

THE BIG WHY

This is why we need a New Testament church. This is why we need brothers and sisters in Christ. We share our anointings when we get together, and the *mutual faith we share comforts*, strengthens, and encourages us all. There is a divine strengthening that takes place when we come together as a body. Paul speaks of being "comforted together." The words *comforted together* come from the Greek word *somparakaleo*, and it means "to comfort jointly or together, two people who comfort each other." It encompasses the idea of teamwork; it says that two or more are more capable than one person alone. Paul says, "I'm praying that God will give me a prosperous journey to get to where you are so I can impart a spiritual gift; this gift will make it better both for you and for me."

God does mathematical calculations on a different level than we do. We would say that if "one puts a thousand to flight, then two will put two thousand to flight." But it's not the same with God. "If one puts a thousand to flight, two will put ten thousand to flight:"

> *How should one chase a thousand, and two put ten thousand to flight, except their Rock had sold them, and the LORD had shut them up? For their rock is not as our Rock, even our enemies themselves being judges.*
>
> *Deuteronomy 32:30-31*

The point here is that if two of God's children come together, their strength is not just the summation of the strengths of each. Something takes place in God so that the combined strength working together is even greater than both individual strengths working apart. The word we'd use for that is *synergism*, which means "the interaction of elements that when combined produce a total effect that is greater than the sum of the individual elements, contributions, etc." You are 10,000 times stronger when you are united with a strong Christian believer!

No wonder the enemy fights God's people from coming together. No wonder Hebrews 10:25 tells us to continue "the assembling of ourselves together, as the manner of some is;...exhorting one another: and so much the more, as ye see the day approaching." This is how God does things! This is the God-kind of comfort—support, encouragement, and strength. The enemy does not want us to receive this; he does not want us to recognize the power of coming together and experiencing a group anointing, strengthening, and comfort.

Somparakaleo is the kind of comfort that can strengthen people who have just had their hearts broken and have decided that they will never ever fall in love with anybody again. Who hasn't heard someone say that before? They had really been hurt for whatever reason, and had made up their minds that they are never going to fall in love again. They're going to remain single for the rest of ther lives.

Imagine a brokenhearted man sitting in a café drinking a cup of cappuccino, when some Christian woman, who attends the same church, walks up and says, "Hi, how are you doing?"

"Fine," he answers.

The Christian sister says, "I don't know what it is, but I've been praying for you. I just want you to know that."

Mr. Brokenhearted can't even remember her name, so he's thinking, *Uh, I don't even know her name; and she's been praying for me!* They end up talking about his situation on a perfectly appropriate Christian level. It just happens to be comparable to something she has experienced.

THE BIG WHY

To make a long story short, both of them end up receiving some very good counsel. Comforted together—two people sit together, talk, and become stronger. They stop focusing on where they came from and feeling so alone in their struggle, and start focusing on where they're going. The devil wants to isolate us from other Christians because he is aware of our synergy when we come together. This is why we need godly, Spirit-filled friends and churches. There is comfort when we're with other believers that will lead to beauty, joy, praise, and restoration. Difficult circumstances can not stop your dreams from happening. Only your own apathy, tears, inactivity, and lack of hope can stop your dreams. Comfort releases your dreams so they can happen!

Have you ever just been driving down the road when you thought of someone and you just had to call them? "Man, I just want you to know that you've been on my mind. I'm praying for you and I bless you." You weren't out to get anything from this person; but, rather, God might even have given you a word of encouragement to deliver to him. That's what that word *somparakaleo* means in Romans 1:12. It's amazing how the Spirit of God can work if He can get someone to cooperate with Him. He said that we will be *comforted together.*

Cindy and I were on vacation in Hawaii a while back. I enjoy going to Hawaii, so Cindy tolerates it and comes with me. My daughters and I really like it over there, but Cindy likes places where it snows, like New York. So, for Cindy's sake, once or twice a year we travel to where it is cold. Then, to satisfy the rest of us, we will go where the weather is nice and warm, even hot. That's the way we do it. So we've solved our differences right there, but some families just fight and fight over where they're going to spend their vacation. I take two vacations. If the one geared specifically for Cindy isn't where it's cold enough, she makes us take three vacations.

So we were in Hawaii, and I saw a plane overhead carrying parachute jumpers. While I consider myself a relatively brave person, I have no intentions of ever parachuting out of an airplane unless it is absolutely necessary. For those who do enjoy doing this, that's their business, and I commend them for having the nerve to do something like that. I watch people who dare to do extreme things on TV sometimes. While I think that it's really cool, I'm still not going to do it. I don't even care if my daddy threatens, "Walter Glenn, if you don't jump, I'm going to throw you out" —*he will be the one who gets thrown out.*

When a beginner gets ready to jump out of the airplane, the instructor straps himself to the new student. The instructor pulls the cord with him, works with him as he maneuvers through the air and positions him just right to land—he experiences the whole process with him. That illustrates exactly what that word *somparakaleo* means—Jesus is going to go with us. He will be strapped to us. Even better, He is *in* us; and we are *in* Him. He said that He will comfort us *together*, all the way.

This reminds me of a story. A husband and wife went to the country fair, and helicopter rides were being offered for fifty dollars. So the husband says to the wife, "Hey, why don't we go up in that helicopter?"

She said, "It's fifty dollars. That's way too much money. I'm not doing it."

So the next year they came back, and the helicopter rides were being offered again. They still cost $50. The husband says, "Come on, honey; let's go up in that helicopter!"

"I'm telling you that I'm not going in that helicopter; you can forget about it," was her reply.

This went on year after year until finally the pilot himself got tired of it. So he said to the couple, "Listen, I'll let you ride for free if you will just get in this helicopter, be quiet, and don't say a word. But if you get up there and you say one word, it's going to cost you fifty dollars." After a little more coaxing, the couple accepts the offer for a free helicopter ride. They get up into the air, and they don't say a word. The pilot does his thing, making big turns this way and that way, *swooping* the helicopter all around—actually *trying* to get the couple to say something. But they don't say a word. Finally the pilot lands the helicopter turns and looks behind him, and finds only the wife sitting there. He asks, "Hey, where's your husband?"

The wife responds, "He fell out the very first time that you made that big swoop."

The pilot asks, "Why didn't you say something?"

The wife said, "That's fifty dollars; that's too much money!"

Aren't we blessed! The Holy Spirit will go with us *all the way!*

Comfort for the New Testament Church

First Corinthians 14:1-3 points out why "prophecy" is so necessary in the Church today. Prophecy is not only strongly encouraged for the Church, as in 1 Corinthians 14:1—"desire spiritual gifts, but rather that ye may prophesy"—but it is for *all* members of the Church. Notice that through prophecy there is a release of divine comfort. The following scripture references bear these two points out:

*I would that ye all spake with tongues [in reference to a message
in tongues that is to be interpreted as opposed to praying in
tongues], but rather that ye prophesied..."*

1 Corinthians 14:5

Wherefore, brethren, covet to prophesy...

1 Corinthians 14:39

*For ye may all prophesy one by one, that all may learn, and all
may be comforted.*

1 Corinthians 14:31

We see here that prophecy is definitely part of God's plan for His
Church. With prophecy being used to bring comfort, we can see that
comfort is definitely a part of God's plan for His Church, as well.
Amazingly and unfortunately, comfort is one of the main ministries
of the Spirit of God that's missing in the Church. So often, we do not
expect or look for this divine ministry of the Holy Spirit. If we dare to
expect or look for anything close to this, our poor substitute is often
exhilaration.

We look for exhilaration. We look for goose bumps. If coming into
the house of God was all about getting spiritual goose bumps, I'd have a
great big block of ice in the front foyer of our church so people could sit
on it until they got their goose-bump thrill. Then they could say, "Wow,
we had a good time in church!" But the problem with this is that we
have to leave the church building, and when we do, we get in our hot
'ole car and can end up more disturbed than ever.

Comfort is a significant provision for the Church, and prophecy
is one of God's primary instruments for delivering this comfort. It is

important that we understand this gift of the Spirit so we will not miss how God wants to use it on our behalf. Prophecy helps you turn your past failures into *lessons*, not shackles, so you are more informed on how you can succeed in your fuure—what a comfort!

Comfort and Prophecy

Again, 1 Corinthians 14:3 says, "But he that prophesieth speaketh unto men to edification, and exhortation, and comfort." Prophecy is divine utterance in a known tongue as opposed to the gift of different kinds of tongues, which is divine utterance in an unknown language.

The Greek word for "comfort" in this verse is *par mutheomy*. It's another one of those beautiful words. It means "to relate or speak a tale, a story, a parable, an example, a type." It also means *to encourage*. It even carries a thought of fiction. So we need to understand that when Paul said, "But he that prophesieth speaketh unto men to…comfort," that particular word "comfort" means to declare something in a parable, in a tale—to relate a story.

Let's illustrate how this works. For example, the Spirit of the Lord might say through an individual "Just like God caused the walls of Jericho to fall down, the Lord says, 'Those walls that are holding back your blessing are going to fall down.'" That would be a prophecy, spoken by the Holy Spirit, relating a story or a type (something that represents something else). Another example could be the Holy Spirit saying through an individual, "Just like birds that take to the sky, those problems in your life are going to take wings and fly away." Again, that would be relating a tale, a story, or a type of something.

One of the best examples of this is Jesus. Again and again, His stories and tales brought comfort, reassurance, cheer, relief, support, and encouragement. His parables had a message of significance for the people He spoke with. Some examples are:

Ye are the salt of the earth: but if the salt have lost his savour, wherewith shall it be salted? it is thenceforth good for nothing, but to be cast out, and to be trodden under foot of men. Ye are the light of the world. A city that is set on an hill cannot be hid. Neither do men light a candle, and put it under a bushel, but on a candlestick; and it giveth light unto all that are in the house. Let your light so shine before men, that they may see your good works, and glorify your Father which is in heaven.

Matthew 5:13-16

Behold the fowls of the air: for they sow not, neither do they reap, nor gather into barns; yet your heavenly Father feedeth them. Are ye not much better than they?

Matthew 6:26

And why take ye thought for raiment? Consider the lilies of the field, how they grow; they toil not, neither do they spin: And yet I say unto you, That even Solomon in all his glory was not arrayed like one of these.

Matthew 6:28-29

"See that sparrow. Don't you think that you're worth more to God than that? Look at that lily of the field over there. Don't you think God will clothe you better than He'll clothe that?" Jesus did this over and over—He related stories that were representative of things, events, or situations. He gave everyone who heard Him answers, support, encouragement, and comfort of some kind. Jesus operated in the gifts of the Spirit; of course, that included the gift of prophecy that brings comfort to the body of Christ.

Prophecy is on a different level than mere words of encouragement; it will have an anointing of God's Spirit on it. "He that prophesieth speaketh unto men to edification." *Edify* means to build up. Prophecy ought to build us up—it ought to charge us up. We can see what edification is like with an example of the battery. I used to own a battery wholesale and retail company. We would buy tractor trailer loads of new batteries at a time. We had several delivery trucks that would go out and bring back old batteries in exchange. Then we'd clean them up and put them on what we called gang chargers, where they would be filled up with electrolyte. We would let them sit there and slowly trickle charge, because if they slowly lost their charge then we could slowly build them back up. This process was called high grading. To get the battery back up to its fullest charge was called *edification*—the same word used in 1 Corinthinans 14:3 in regard to prophecy.

Building up, edifying, encouraging. A good illustration of how this works is a father who is encouraging his child to succeed, even exceed his or her limits, to go beyond his or her fears. I remember when my daughter Catherine was a little girl. Cindy and I had three girls, and I was always encouraging them to do boy's stuff like basketball and track, because I didn't have a son to do this with.

Now my wife was the head baton-twirler in high school. She even used fire batons. Our girls would plead, "Momma, do your baton thing." She'd do the baton thing, and I'd say, "Don't do that. They'll grow up to be little sissy girls. Get 'em a football helmet, you know." But that didn't work.

So, anyway, my daughter Catherine decided to run track. When I was in school, I ran the 400 meter and the 200 meter—and it was like adrenaline city. When you're out there, it's just you and the rest of the runners. Even though you don't know if you've got what it takes and you're scared, and your heart is pounding in your chest, *you can't wait to run.* Even though part of you wants to quit, when that starter gun goes off, *you run*—you explode on the inside—and give it everything you've got. It's the same thing for little girls in a track meet. I remember when Catherine first started running track. She said, "Well, Daddy, it's just scary. I'm on that starting line; and… and I'm just scared."

I said, "Now, honey, I want you to listen to me. That adrenaline you're feeling, that's like gasoline on a fire. That's like an energy juice that God put on the inside of you. It's not something to be afraid of. That emotion, that feeling is actually what can propel you to do what you can't do when you're just normally out there running or jogging. It'll energize you. It'll give you extra energy and extra speed and all of that. So when you feel that coming on, and you're feeling all of that fear, as well, know this: that's not something to cause you to shut down; you're supposed to embrace that. God put that on the inside of you. Then you'll feel like, *Man, I'm going to do better than I've ever done.*" I would encourage Catherine to go beyond her fear and to succeed. I would exhort her. I would prophesy.

We don't have to be prophesied over by someone else. The Spirit of God can talk to us directly. It is okay if somebody else speaks to us on behalf of God, but the Spirit of God can actually talk to us and say, *You can do all things through Christ who strengthens you. Why do you think you can't do something? Just because you haven't done it before doesn't mean you can't do it now. If I told you to do it, you can do it. Start that jail ministry!*

THE BIG WHY

Begin that new business! Step out. Pray for that person on the job! That's the Spirit of God. That's not the devil talking to us. If God confirms it through someone else, that's okay. He might just do that.

There is a time and place for God to use prophecy—just like I was speaking to my daughter, adding a degree of comfort, motivating her to go beyond her limits. (Keep in mind that prophecy will have the anointing of God's Spirit.) But prophecy, like anything else, can be abused. One of the main tactics of the enemy is to take something that is of God and get people to either overemphasize or underemphasize its usefulness, appeal, or authority. When something is abused, people tend to back away from it altogether. This must be the enemy's plan when it comes to prophecy—because a comfortless, discouraged, mourning Church presents little to no threat to his agenda. I will share a few words of caution when it comes to this tremendously important gift of the Spirit.

For starters, because of Jesus' work on Calvary, we no longer have to depend on someone else to hear from God. We can hear God for ourselves. That is not to say that God will not use someone else on occasion, like a prophet. I firmly believe in the prophetic ministry, but it's important that we not become *dependent* on other people to hear from God. When we do that, we are putting ourselves in the dangerous situation of being manipulated and controlled by someone else.

God most assuredly wants to talk to us and help us in our decisions, but prophetic dependency is incorrect. Prophecy really should only confirm what God has spoken to an individual earlier, though on rare occasions a prophet may speak something new. For example, the prophet may warn someone of approaching danger or that he is about to miss God in some way. Sometimes God has personally been trying to get a message to an individual, but for some reason that individual hasn't listened. That's when God in His mercy can move through the gift of prophecy to get His message across. The individual should follow up directly with God. That prophecy, like all others, should be judged to determine if it is true.

We should never live our lives based on prophecy alone. If someone comes up to us and says, "Thus saith the Lord, thou must go to Uganda," we had better go get a word from God *ourselves* or else take that "prophet" with us so we'll know when to come home.

God does speak through prophets and through prophecy, but more often He will speak directly to our spirit through His Word and through the Holy Spirit. This is especially true when He uses the Holy Spirit to warn us of impending danger.

God does not lead the Church by prophecy alone. I believe that is why the Apostle Paul, in 1 Corinthians 14, veers us away from having services of nothing but prophecies. He is quite plain about this: "Let the prophets speak two or three" (v. 29). He is saying that at the most we should have three prophecies. "Prophesying serveth not for them that believe not, but for them which believe" (v. 22). In other words, there is an order in God's spiritual program, as Paul makes clear: "Let all things be done decently and in order" (v. 40).

Paul isn't getting rid of anything here. All he is doing in the book of First Corinthians is correcting the abuse. He never discounts or eliminates any of the ministries of the Holy Spirit; he just puts them in order. I've said for years that the book of First Corinthians ought to be called the book of First Corrections, because in almost every chapter Paul corrects an abuse of some kind or something going on in the church. But Paul never eliminates anything except when he talks about sin.

He is not blackballing the spiritual gift of prophecy, but merely putting it in its place. He is veering us away from wrongly depending on it. He doesn't want us to allow prophets and prophecy to guide the Church, because Jesus is still the head of the Church and He speaks to us primarily through the Word and the Holy Spirit. There is a difference between God using the prophet and our becoming dependent upon the prophet. The prophetic should never be the only focus or even the main focus of the assembly. If it is, there is a problem. On the other hand, if prophecy never occurs in our church services, then that is a problem, as well.

In my thirty years of being in ministry in one capacity or another, I personally have had given to me many "words from the Lord" by other people; however, I can probably count on both hands the ones that I claimed, that I felt in my spirit were from God. The others, for the most part, were probably from well-meaning people, but I did not sense an anointing on their messages indicating that they were from God. I mean, I didn't turn the table over, get up, and walk off in a fit of rage. If the word wasn't something bad, I'd say, "Well, praise the Lord. Well, Sister, glory to God. Thank God for His gifts. Let's see if this is real." But I didn't blindly acccept that their prophecy was actually from God when it came to what all these people had to say.

When something is from God, it should confirm what is already in our spirits. First John 2:20 tells us: "But ye have an unction from the Holy One." And 1 John 2:27 says, "But the anointing which ye have received of him abideth in you, and ye need not that any man teach you." If we read, "Ye need not that any man teach you," in context,

John is saying that other people don't have to tell us what is from God and what isn't. Even though we may not understand everything about something—like a word—we should still have a knowing in our spirits, if it is truly from God.

Nevertheless, God does use personal prophecy, and I am not resistant if someone confirms something I already know in my spirit. I am happy to receive it, and grateful, but no one will ever take the place of God's voice in my own heart.

I call prophecy an "entry level" gift in the gifts of the Spirit. "For ye may all prophesy" (1 Corinthians 14:31). As such, it is an instrument that God has chosen to deliver *comfort* to the body of Christ. Though we have seen an overabundance of prophecies and wrong dependence—or abuse—upon this gift, there are genuine prophecies that God wants to use, because He wants His Church edified, exhorted, and comforted.

We must continue to desire this gift, even covet this gift, and seek knowledge of this gift—"Now concerning spiritual gifts, brethren, I would not have you ignorant" (1 Corinthians 12:1). We don't know what people around us have been through this week, this month, last year, or throughout their lives. When we meet someone, we need to be quick to edify, exhort and comfort. God will get in our words. We'll be speaking words they'll understand, and the Spirit of God will sometimes turn that into the gift of prophecy.

When we pass people in public, we ought to edify, exhort, and comfort them. When we're walking up and down the hallway in a church, we don't have to know someone's name to be a blessing to them. "My, my, my, tonight you just look better than I've ever seen you before. You look like God is working in your life. Glory to God."

THE BIG WHY

It's amazing how the Holy Spirit will get in that and even turn that into a divine prophecy. That's "Gifts of the Spirit 101". The Word said, "For ye may all prophesy" (1 Corinthians 14:31). May we allow the Spirit of God to comfort us and to comfort *through us* with the gift of prophecy.

Chapter 17

COMFORT AND DESIRE, VISION AND COMMITMENT

When the Holy Spirit is working in our life, the Bible says there will be a divine comfort. The Holy Spirit will minister that to us if we allow it.

COMFORT AND DESIRE

I've already pointed out that Paul, when writing about the gifts of the Spirit, says, "He that prophesieth speaketh unto men to edification, and exhortation, *and comfort*" (1 Corinthians 14:3). Something of special significance that Paul says even before saying this is: "Follow after charity [love], and *desire* spiritual gifts" (1 Corinthians 14:1, emphasis mine). *Desire.* Desire is a huge part of the ministry of the Holy Spirit. We're not going to experience much Holy Spirit activity in our life—including the ministry of comfort—if we do not earnestly desire the ministry of the Holy Spirit. We can go to one church that says, "We believe in the Holy Spirit and the gifts of the Spirit"; and we can go to another church that says the same. What actually happens in these two churches when it comes to evidence of the Spirit working can be miles apart. For instance, in one church people will get healed and in the other they won't. Why is that? *Desire.*

A sweet little lady came up to me one day during a Sunday service, and she asked, "Do you remember me?"

I said, "Yes, ma'am, I do."

She said, "I'm believing God for healing. Do you remember in 2000 when I came here and had liver cancer?"

I said, "Yes, ma'am, I do remember."

She stated, "You know, God healed me of that. I don't have that anymore. I didn't have any of the treatments. God healed me; it's gone. It was a miracle. It's gone." She continued, "I have some gallbladder problems right now, and if God can heal me of cancer, He can heal my gallbladder."

I said, "I agree with you."

She said, "I prefer not to have the surgery. Would you stand in agreement with me for that?" Now, even though I'm sure that God will use medicine, doctors, and treatments to heal (I recommend regular checkups with your physician) it seems that there are many times when people are healed through prayer and faith.

I said, "I'll pray with you right now. If you have faith to get healed of cancer, I believe you can get healed of gallbladder problems, too." I also encouraged her to verify her physical healing with her physicians.

Why does one church experience healings when they say, "I believe in healing and miracles"; and then, another church says the same thing, but they have no healings? The key word here is "desire." That is why it's important when we come to the house of God that we *pull* in the Spirit. It is even more important that we pull *together*. That's what desire is— *pulling*. God will, in response to that, pour out an anointing, like a healing anointing. Then the gift of the working of miracles or the gifts of healing will begin to happen. This woman had a strong, godly desire to be healed by the Holy Spirit, and she pursued that healing in faith and wisdom.

I remember something that happened in our church two different times over a period of ten years. During one of those times, I was preaching in a church service when the Holy Spirit spoke to me. Now I like old cars, and it so happened that I had a Mustang. It was *real* nice, white, and with a T-top. It was a pretty cool car. At the time I had three of them. The Spirit of the Lord said to me, *There's a young man sitting over there. Give him that car.*

I thought, *I sure hope this is God.* So I said to the young man, "In the Name of Jesus, I just give you that car." The man was attending college and needed a car to be able to go to church, attend his classes, and go to work.

That night, the desire of God got in several other people the same way. That's the best way that I can explain it. I believe three or four more cars were given away to people in that service. People in the congregation just started giving away cars. I remember another night I gave away a nice Rolex watch to a gentleman in church. By the end of the service, a dozen or so people had given away watches. The desire of God just got in people and they started giving.

Some people might say, "Well, what's the big deal about that?"

For one, they would be surprised to know how many watches I have *now*. God moves in the principles of sowing and reaping. I believe that *desiring* the ministry of the Holy Spirit—which includes comfort—leads to these kinds of things happening in our church services and in our individual lives. Desire is a huge thing when it comes to seeing God move on our behalf.

Desire has to do with change—changing from one situation to the next. We go from not being healed to being healed, from not being saved to being saved, from not seeing the Spirit of God move to seeing Him move, and from being mournful to being comforted. Are we getting the point? Jesus calls this "hungering and thirsting," as in "Blessed are they which do hunger and thirst after righteousness: for they shall be filled" (Matthew 5:6). Whatever you truly desire is what you pursue in life.

Desire has to do with change, because desire is essential for change to take place. It is possible for something good to happen without us actively desiring it. We may have wanted the thing to happen and have given up on getting it. The lame man by the Gate Beautiful in Acts 3 was not expecting—*pulling*—to be healed the day he asked Peter for alms. Instead Peter responded by saying, "Silver and gold have I none; but such as I have give I thee: In the Name of Jesus Christ of Nazareth rise up and walk" (v. 6). Someone who is serious and smart about his or her life does not settle for hits and misses—what will be, will be. God puts a high premium on desire. He responds to spiritual hunger. "For he satisfieth the longing soul, and filleth the hungry soul with goodness" (Psalm 107:9). He wants us to want Him and His will. His will is all about wholeness, soundness, peace, and comfort, the God-kind of comfort.

To experience comfort in the place of mourning is a God-given desire. We should not misunderstand Paul's words in Philippians 4:11, where he says, "Not that I speak in respect of want: for I have learned, in whatsoever state I am, therewith to be content." Paul is not telling us here to stop desiring something better. He is not telling us to pretend that everything is okay, when really it is not. He is not telling us to settle for anything that is less than God's best for us. I believe he is speaking of a contentment here that comes with knowing that God wants us to have abundant life; and, therefore, we can expect Him to bring us through our present—even undesirable—situation. Godly contentment is learned, not earned!

Misunderstanding scriptures such as Philippians 4:11 has caused us to kill God-given desires and desiring *period*. Since God cares about our whole man—spirit, soul, and body, according to 1 Thessalonians 5:23—when we kill our desire, we kill our urge to attain what we *should* be desiring. We become passive; we become defeated. The devil wins! Hasn't he taken enough from us? Winners are people who don't just ask *why* they fell down, they keep getting up!

It's time to desire again. Luke 6:21 says, "Blessed are ye that hunger now: for ye shall be filled. Blessed are ye that weep now: for ye shall laugh." It's time to laugh—to take off the garment of ashes, mourning, and heaviness and be comforted, to bring on beauty, joy, and praise.

It's time for rivers to be opened in "high places, and fountains in the midst of the valleys," and for the wilderness to be made "a pool of water, and the dry land springs of water" (Isaiah 41:18). Why? Because we have been "poor and needy," and we sought water, and our tongue has failed for thirst—*we have desired*. (Isaiah 41:17.) Desire has its reward: "I the LORD will hear them, I the God of Israel will not forsake them" (v. 17).

VISION VILLAINS—DREAM DESTROYERS

In the Old Testament, the Prophet Habakkuk talks about vision right before the chapter when he takes his "neginoth" and gives God some "Shigionoth"—*taking his musical instrument and giving God some praise*. There are people reading this book who are going through things right now or may have to face something tomorrow that is very challenging or discouraging. What I will share next will cause them to have the victory every single time.

In Habakkuk, chapter 2, Habakkuk talks about vision and how necessary it is.

> *I will stand upon my watch, and set me upon the tower, and will watch to see what he will say unto me, and what I shall answer when I am reproved. And the LORD answered me, and said, Write the vision, and make it plain upon tables, that he may run that readeth it. For the vision is yet for an appointed time, but at the end it shall speak, and not lie: though it tarry, wait for it; because it will surely come, it will not tarry.*
>
> *Habakkuk 2:1-3*

Vision plays a huge role in experiencing God's comfort—including courage and boldness for the battle, and beauty, joy, and praise for our lives. Before the Prophet Habakkuk could even begin to write the vision, he had to "stand upon [his] watch," taking time to look and listen for what God would say. We must take time away from the hurry and flurry of our lives so that we can hear God's voice. The "tower" in Habakkuk 1 is representative of finding a place "above" the sights and sounds of what's happening around us: "And thine ears shall hear a word behind thee, saying, This is the way, walk ye in it, when ye turn to the right hand, and when ye turn to the left" (Isaiah 30:21).

Habakkuk has a lot of complaints to make in the verses ahead in Habakkuk, chapter 2. Too many people find enough time to complain to God, but little or no time to sincerely watch and listen for what He has to say. Never let complaining become a substitute for solving problems.

Lacking vision, particularly God's vision, is a dangerous thing. Proverbs 29:18 tells us, "Where there is no vision, the people perish." If we do not have our own vision, we are more likely to adopt the vision that other people have for us. Our circumstances or our five senses could dictate our vision, and it could be a far cry from the plan and purpose that God has in mind for our lives.

Habakkuk talks about the importance of a vision and then talks about things that can steal visions. In Habakkuk 2:6, he talks about dishonest people who try to distort and steal people's God-focus and the vision He has given them: "Shall not all these take up a parable against him, and a taunting proverb against him, and say, Woe to him that increaseth that which is not his! how long? and to him that ladeth himself with thick clay!" We can be moving forward, trying to do something good and knowing that we're following God's plan; and then, all of a sudden, somebody dishonest—a thief—steps in and attempts to detour God's plan for our lives. That happens!

Once, through study and prayer, I felt very moved to buy a tract of seemingly useless land. I felt so strongly that I should buy it that I paid a million dollars for it. Some people I knew in our church became so distracted from the vision to develop that land that they talked very negatively about us and finally left the church after influencing several others to quit. I continued to pursue the vision of that property for a few months and then sold that same tract of land for four million dollars! Vision takes time, vision is a process, vision takes work. But only vision can come to pass. It's your future success coming at you twenty-four hours at a time. Embrace it, work it, pray for it—remember, you will become it.

THE BIG WHY

Habakkuk 2:9 talks about greedy people who, for evil gain, try to stop the vision: "Woe to him that coveteth an evil covetousness to his house, that he may set his nest on high, that he may be delivered from the power of evil!" God has a plan for our lives; but our adversary, the devil, has a plan of attack to prevent that plan from ever happening. Our vision, along with the comfort that comes from knowing God's vision, positions us for power through the ministry of the Holy Spirit over and over again.

In verse 12, Habakkuk talks about the hypocrites who are trying to take from him and build their own empires contrary to the plan of God: "Woe to him that buildeth a town with blood, and stablisheth a city by iniquity!" For example, some people set out to murder the reputations of others to advance their own cause. God calls this an abomination in Proverbs 6:16-19:

> *These six things doth the LORD hate: yea, seven are an*
> *abomination unto him: a proud look, a lying tongue, and*
> *hands that shed innocent blood, an heart that deviseth wicked*
> *imaginations, feet that be swift in running to mischief, a false*
> *witness that speaketh lies, and he that soweth discord among*
> *brethren.*

In verse 15, Habakkuk talks about drunkenness, pornography, drugs, and all of the sin and moral issues that can stop our visions and God's comfort: " Woe unto him that giveth his neighbour drink, that puttest thy bottle to him, and makest him drunken also, that thou mayest look on their nakedness!" This verse says "woe to him" who tries to get his neighbor to sin, who tries to morally weaken him and make him vulnerable in any way to the enemy's attack.

Habakkuk goes on in verse 19: "Woe unto him that saith to the wood, Awake; to the dumb stone, Arise, it shall teach! Behold, it is laid over with gold and silver, and there is no breath at all in the midst of it." Habakkuk essentially says, "There is an attempt to stop the vision. Idolatry, false religions, cults, and false ideologies are trying to rise up." The thief can come in the guise of religion and devotion, but it is idolatrous and can steal one's vision. Excessive or blind adoration, reverence, and devotion come in different packages. A person's ministry can become his idol and can cause him to act cruelly towards other Christians in order to "get to the top." Ambition gone wrong will prey upon the anointings of others to promote its vision. God wants us to know that there are vision thieves. Go where your vision is accepted. Vision requires effort and partnership. True friends admire vision, they do not try to block it. Vision comforts!

Always be an encourager of vision in other people. In the Bible, Joseph had a vision that finally came to pass, but his brothers were jealous of it. (Genesis 37; 39-47.) Jealous people are dangerous people. In the Old Testament, the Prophet Daniel was a helper of three Hebrew childrens' visions and he began a pathway of promotion that, even though he was a captive, promoted him to a rank similar to a prime minister in the land. (Daniel 1-2.) Vision always promotes.

COMFORT AND COMMITMENT

Sometimes our thoughts, words, and actions tell God, "God, I know that there's a future out there for me; but I just don't *feel* like it." The Bible doesn't say we are to feel our way in God. It says, "For we walk by faith, not by sight" (2 Corinthians 5:7). It says, "Commit thy way unto the LORD; trust also in him; and he shall bring it to pass" (Psalm

37:5). It says, "Trust in the LORD with all thine heart; and lean not unto thine own understanding. In all thy ways acknowledge him, and he shall direct thy paths" (Proverbs 3:5-6).

If we commit all of our ways to God, He will direct our paths. We can trust Him to properly execute our plans, but *we have to commit* our plans to Him. If we can learn the power of commitment—committing our ways to God so He can direct our paths—we will have God's best, including His divine comfort. Refuse to be distracted from your vision. Stay strong through prayer, planning, people, and pathway. Be sure these four things are part of your commitment and comfort will come to you because you are doing all you can.

Chapter 18

COMFORT AND
THE MINISTRY OF ANGELS

I used to think that comfort was simply a matter of God trying to make me feel better during a difficult time. I found out that comfort is much more than that—it is very anointed and it has Holy Spirit power in it. I shared that God's desire to minister comfort to us is one of the key ways that the Holy Spirit's ministry of angels is released.

I believe our need for comfort motivates our Lord to release the ministry of angels as much and as quickly as anything else. He is moved when we have reason for mourning, grief, sorrow, and pain, since He Himself is acquainted with rejection, sorrow, grief, oppression, affliction, agony, and more. (Isaiah 53:2,3,7, 11.) He is acquainted with tears. He wept at Lazarus' grave, and Hebrews 5:7 and 8 says of Him,

Who in the days of his flesh, when he had offered up prayers and
supplications with strong crying and tears unto him that was able
to save him from death, and was heard in that he feared; though
he were a Son, yet learned he obedience by the things which he
suffered.

Our God is moved with compassion, and sometimes we may experience the ministry of angels to comfort us.

THE POWER OF ANGELS

The Bible says that angels are powerful ministering spirits that are sent out in the service of God to assist those who are to inherit salvation. "Are they not all ministering spirits, sent forth to minister for them who shall be heirs of salvation?" (Hebrews 1:14). It is very interesting that from the time of Jesus in the Garden of Gethsemane—right before salvation is possible—we see in the Bible an escalation of angelic activity in the earth. This is even more true when we see what is yet to happen in the book of Revelation.

In the Garden of Gethsemane, when the soldiers came to arrest Jesus, though He already knew what was going on, He asked them, "Whom seek ye?" (John 18:4). When they told Him, "Jesus of Nazareth," He said, "I am he" (v. 5). Immediately "they went backward, and fell to the ground" (v. 6). When they got up, Jesus asked them again who they were seeking, and they said again, "Jesus of Nazareth" (v. 7). This time He let them stay standing.

It is significant that in the Greek, the "he" in verse 5 is in italics, meaning that Jesus actually said to the soldiers, "I am." When Moses asked God what he should tell the Israelites was His name, God said, "I AM THAT I AM…say unto the children of Israel, I AM hath sent me unto you" (Exodus 3:14). What Jesus was actually saying to the soldiers was: "You really think you've come to arrest me? I'm the King of kings; I created everything. Don't you know that my Father could send right now more than twelve legions of angels and set me free?" (Matthew 26:53.)

A "legion" is a division of the Roman army and can comprise up to six thousand soldiers. Twelve legions would be seventy-two thousand soldiers—or seventy-two thousand angels in Jesus' case. So Jesus was saying, "Don't you know God could send seventy-two thousand angels?" I can't help but think of seventy-two thousand angels watching Jesus mocked and beaten when He went before the high priest, in Pilate's hall, and on His way to Calvary. I think of seventy-two thousand angels looking on, hoping that the Creator will say, "Come get Me"; but instead He said, "You little soldiers think you are going to mess with me? If I just move my finger, it can be all over." Then Jesus let them take Him, "that the scriptures of the prophets might be fulfilled" (Matthew 26:56).

We read in Isaiah 37:36, "Then the angel of the LORD went forth, and smote in the camp of the Assyrians a hundred and fourscore and five thousand: and when they arose early in the morning, behold, they were all dead corpses." One angel of the Lord killed 185,000 men in one night. I've done the math for the purpose of this teaching. If we multiply 185,000 dead corpses by 72,000 angels, we have 13,320,000,000 dead corpses from that many angels. Jesus was saying that He could call 72,000 angels and wipe out 13,320,000,000 people.

But instead of wiping humanity out, Jesus chose to die and wipe out all of their sins. To experience the benefit of this, all they had to do was accept His cleansing and forgiveness through faith.

ANGELS AND HEIRS OF SALVATION

The ministry of angels is incredibly strong, and let's not forget that they are sent by God "to minister for them who shall be heirs of salvation" (Hebrews 1:14). Let's go a little further with this. According to Scripture, we become an heir when we get born again. You and I become children of God. Very simply, all we have to do is "believe on the Lord Jesus Christ, and thou shalt be saved" (Acts 16:31). Let's look at what Jesus said in John 1:12. "But as many as received him [Jesus], to them gave he power *to become* the sons of God, even to them that believe on his name" (emphasis mine). But there is a difference between being something positionally and becoming that something experientally. Being something and actually experiencing something are two different things.

Paul makes reference to Christians who are living beneath their inheritance: "Now I say, That the heir, as long as he is a child, differeth nothing from a servant, though he be lord of all" (Galatians 4:1). We have a different heirship in our lives when the Holy Spirit is working in us. Acts 1:8 tells us that we "shall receive power, after that the Holy Ghost is come upon [us]." Jesus said in John 1:12 that He has given us *power* to become the sons of God. Being filled with the Holy Spirit gives us power to *experience* what is rightfully ours—our inheritance— as children of God.

Romans 8 has additional things to say about this: "For as many as are led by the Spirit of God, they are the sons of God....The Spirit itself beareth witness with our spirit, that we are the children of God: And if children, then heirs; heirs of God, and joint-heirs with Christ" (vv. 14, 16-17). Being led by God's Spirit, and therefore getting to be the sons of God that we are—allows us to truly experience our inheritance with Christ.

According to Acts 1:8 there is a power that we can receive; angels are just waiting to help minster that power in the eleven ways I have shared. There is an anointed power in the Holy Spirit for destroying every yoke. (Isaiah 10:27.) The yokes of grief, sorrow, pain, sickness, poverty, and mourning can become agents of oppression, subjection, servitude—things that bind us. Our bad choices or the devil may have yoked us to things that hurt us.

Isaiah 10:27 says that the anointing *destroys* the yoke. It causes the yoke to deteriorate, disintegrate, decompose—to become weak to the point of falling apart and breaking off. The anointing is God's power for our particular assignment. If something that doesn't look like God, sound like God, smell like God, taste like God, or feel like God tries to yoke itself to us, we can mark it down that it is our assignment to get rid of it. The anointing of God's power will begin to destroy the chains that bind our lives. We must remember that sometimes God will use angels to get the job done.

PART SIX

GOD'S CROWNING GLORY

Chapter 19

ANGELA'S OPUS

The devil has underestimated God every step of the way. His gravest mistake has been underestimating God's wisdom and heart when He created man and made man His crowning glory. Elevating man to this place and counting on him to come through is a move on God's part that Satan, with all the force and fury of hell, would like to make God regret and think was the mistake of His eternal lifetime.

The psalmist says in Psalm 8:4-8,

What is man that thou art mindful of him? and the son of man, that thou visitest him? For thou hast...crowned him with glory and honour. Thou madest him to have dominion over the works of thy hands; thou hast put all things under his feet: All sheep and oxen, yea, and the beasts of the field; the fowl of the air, and the fish of the sea, and whatsoever passeth through the paths of the seas.

God glories—exults with triumph, rejoices proudly—in everything that He has done. The earth declares the glory of God. The heavens declare the glory of God.

"When I consider thy heavens, the work of thy fingers, the moon and the stars, which thou hast ordained..." (Psalm 8:3). The psalmist goes on to say that after he has considered the heavens—"your macro-skies, dark and enormous, your handmade sky-jewelry, moon and stars mounted in their settings" (Psalm 8:3 MSG)—then "I look at my micro-self [man] and wonder, Why do you bother with us? Why take a second look our way?" (v. 4 MSG). The earth is filled with God's glory, and the heavens are filled with God's glory, yet Psalm 8 says that *man* is God's crowning glory. The greatest way that God can be glorified is by His shining in and through lives.

Because of sin, the devil thought he had dealt a major blow to God's aspirations and expectations of His human creations. As my dear Irish minister friend, Hassan Boyle, shared at Angela's Homegoing Celebration:

> *A bird glories in its flight. A fish glories in an ocean where it can swim. A seed glories in the ground where it can grow up to be a tree. You put that bird in a cage; and although it has the potential to glory, it doesn't. You put that fish in a bowl; and although it has the potential to glory, it doesn't. You put that seed in a bag; and although it has the potential to glory, it doesn't. You put man under sin; and although he has the potential to glory, he doesn't. But when Jesus sets you free, you can do what others cannot do. You can glory. God can personify. God can use you to let a generation know that He lives.*

God made man His crowning glory. He made man His ultimate triumph—the number one way through which He Himself would be glorified, because man can *choose* to love Him. God's other creatures go by instinct. Birds don't choose to love or glorify God. The fish and the lions don't choose to love or glorify God. But man can choose to do both.

God chose first. He loved first. He created us with this in mind—He chose to love us, and even before we sinned, He had already planned that Jesus would die for our sins so we could be restored to Him. There *are* those of His created beings who have and who will continue *to choose* to love Him back.

There have been lovers of God in every age, individuals and groups here and there. But this is the Lord's most glorious hour on this earth and its most glorious hour for showing His power and majesty. We are also facing the most inglorious hour of the enemy's demonic assault. Both good and evil are coming to a head. We are coming to a time of extremes of both good and bad and lovers of God and lovers of evil. It is going to take an extreme and radical generation of lovers of God, like no generation that has come before, to be empowered by God and entrusted with the resources of this world.

Nothing must stand in our way. I believe that God has gone to great lengths to ensure our empowerment through the message of *The Big Why*. There is a generation rising that will not be crippled by fear, ignorance, and disbelief. When all else has failed to stand in the way, the enemy will attempt to get in our face with the final weapon in his arsenal—death itself. But he will be too late!

We will have received the revelation. God's people are not limited to just information. We have received the Spirit of God that searches and knows all the things of God. (1 Corinthians 2:10-12.) We have the advantage.

We have found out that no "unjust weight" misses the all-seeing eye of God, and that *He will recompense*. We have the "heads up" on cults and bad government, on the curse, on lack of diligence, and on evil

THE BIG WHY

spirits. When sorrow and grief have an occasion to cross our paths, we have a prescription from the Great Physician for accessing the divine ministry of comfort. We fill up with beauty, joy, and praise, and a big dose of restoration. Ministering angels make house calls on our behalf. We refuse to be stuck or drifting, but choose to be transformed. We renew our minds as we pull down strongholds of wrong thinking, and then replace wrong thinking with positive thoughts.

We have been given the keys to resist the thief. Death's sting and the grave's victory have been swallowed up by heaven's reality and by faith's greatest triumph that neither death, hell, nor the grave can kill a Christian. Death is only a door of entry for us, a threshold to step over into our new home. We are more alive there than we were here, and we will still not be done with our assignment on earth. Our works will follow and even multiply and go on to something more and greater.

Yes, the devil underestimated God when it came to God's choice to make man His crowning glory. He underestimated God when it came to God's choice to love man and put His "treasure in earthen vessels" (2 Corinthians 4:7). The devil underestimated God when he thought he could get by with his "unjust weight," and illegally invade and violently remove the lives of God's own from the face of the earth. In doing so, the devil thought he had triumphantly aborted anything God had planned to accomplish through His people. The devil underestimated who Angela Hallam and multitudes of others like her were: God's family, His children, sons and daughters of the Most High. One does not spurn the living God and lay his hands on God's own and get by. God will recompense. He will repay.

I believe that now Satan will be able to underestimate those of us who remain on this earth *less than ever*, because we will expect our two-fold, even seven-fold recompense. We will lay hold of restoration as being rightfully ours. We will do this on the authority of God's Word. We are going to "build the old wastes…raise up the former desolations, and…repair the waste cities" (Isaiah 61:4). We refuse to be "a people robbed and spoiled…snared in holes…hid in prison houses…for a prey, and none delivereth; for a spoil, and none saith, Restore" (Isaiah 42:22). From this day forward, we say, *"Restore!"*

God will use us to carry forward the works of those now in heaven, who can not be made perfect without us —who will not see a satisfactory end to what God assigned them to do without our help. When the enemy came to kill, steal, and destroy, he thought he would have the last word, but the innocent ones whose lives he thought he had attacked and stilled will have the last say-so, along with God the Father. Their works will follow, and we will help ensure that they do.

Angela Hallam's works have not come to an end by any stretch of the imagination. Angela expressed her love for God and her passion for evangelism through drama, theater, music and preaching. "The Road to Emmaus" and "Hotel Heartbreak, Hotel Hallelujah" continue to be major productions, live extravaganzas, but they only reflect the bigger production of Angela's life. It was this aesthetic, masterful, commanding, authoritative, and full-of-the-Master opus–a musical, literary, and choreographed life–that continues to grow and rise and surpass the limits of a seventeen-year-old girl's earthly stay. "Angela's Opus" continues to play.

This book is an in-your-face slap to the enemy who viciously targeted her life. This work is inspired by this fiery young woman of God and imbued with her radical love for Him. From the other side of eternity, alive and well, she continues to spur her generation on to fulfill its divine appointment for this day and hour.

"Catherine, you need compassion," Angela told her older sister. It is natural for human beings to want to believe the best about people, trusting their intentions to be good and their motives to be pure. Inadvertently, this can result in believing in people *too much, even in Christians.* This can then lead to being taken advantage of, to being misled and having our trust abused. Because of this, many people are cynical, bitterly distrusting of people *and even of God Himself.* They hold a low opinion of humanity overall. In a world like this, Angela Hallam did not give up on people because her God hadn't given up on them. Her opus is still playing. It beats to the beat of His heart.

> *My name is Angela Hallam. I'm seventeen; and I say this to people all the time and it is so true—and that is why I say it: There is absolutely nothing, nothing in the world better than serving Jesus. No matter what you do in life, no matter how many times you fall, no matter how many times you think you've messed up, God is always there to pick you up and get you right back to where you were, because that's the kind of God He is, and because He loves you just so incredibly much. I am so excited that you made this decision. Don't let anyone ever, ever take you off course, but follow God all the days of your life.*

Angela said this after five hundred people had just walked down the aisle to give their lives to Jesus following the "Heartbreak Hotel, Hotel Hallelujah" stage production at Abundant Life Christian Church. Can we follow Angela's choreography? We only need to fall in line with the footsteps of Jesus.

*I firmly believe that this year we will see the blessings of God
and the windows of heaven opened up and we'll have poured to us
so much that we don't even have room to receive it…individually
as well as at The Chosen. You all, we have a lot to do this year.
We have a lot of people to reach. We have a lot of stuff to build. We
have a lot to buy. We've got a lot of people to get saved.*

This was Angela's message to The Chosen a few days before she went home to be with the Lord. The last thing she told the church before she left: "No matter what, serve God!" A very befitting title for her opus…*I do believe!*

ENDNOTES

Chapter 1: The Glory of Kings

1. "Red hair" www.wikipedia.org. 14 May 2010. <http://cn.wikipedia.org/wiki/Red_hair>

Chapter 5: I Will Recompense

1. "Deaths of the Twelve Apostles" www.wikipedia.org. 19 February 2010. <http://en.wikipedia.org/wiki/Deaths_of_the_Twelve_Apostles.htm>

Chapter 6: Cults and Bad Governments

1. Singer, Dr. Margaret Thaler. "Cults in Our Midst" 19 February 2010. <http://www.factnet.org/singer.htm>

2. Ross, Rick. "Frequently Asked Questions: Defining a Cult" 19 February 2010. <http://www.rickross.com/faq.html>

3. Ibid.

4. "Algerian Civil War" www.wikipedia.org. 19 February 2010 <http://en.wikipedia.org/wiki/Algerian_Civil_War#massacres_and_reconciliation>

5. Ibid.

Additional resources

Strong, James *Strong's Exhaustive Concordance to the Bible.* Peabody, Massachusetts: Hendrickson Publishers, 2007.

Vine, W. E. *Vine's Expository Dictionary of Old and New Testament Words.* Nashville: Thomas Nelson, 1996.

Bullinger, E. W. *Companion Bible: King James Version.* Grand Rapids, Michigan: Kregel Publications, 1974.

Dake, Finis Jennings *Dake Annotated Reference Bible.* Lawrenceville, Georgia: Dake Publishing, 1996.

Websters New World College Dictionary, 3rd Ed. New York: Simon & Schuster, Inc., 1996.

Acknowledgements

Cover Design: Christian Ophus

Editors: Bobbie Jo Hamilton
Lisa DeSpain

ABOUT THE AUTHOR

THE MAN

Pastor Walter Hallam has been actively serving the Lord since his youth. He knew at an early age that God had called him to preach. Still, he ministered as a layman in his local church until 1985. God then placed it in his heart to move with his wife, Cindy and children to Texas City, Texas and begin a church.

Pastor Hallam, a powerful and dynamic speaker, ministers the good news of the Gospel with authority. He operates effectively in the gifts of the Spirit through the gifts of healing, faith, miracles, word of knowledge, word of wisdom, and prophecy. Having a strong apostolic anointing, Pastor Hallam is often referred to as a "pastor to pastors."

Because of the unique ministry outreaches of Abundant Life Christian Center (ALCC), Pastor Walter Hallam has appeared on several national and local television & radio programs to talk about what God is doing through the Body of Christ.

THE MINISTRY

ALCC has become one of the fastest growing churches on the Texas Gulf Coast with over 3,000 members. The ministries of Abundant Life Christian Center include:

- Master's Life – 2-year Bible Training Program

- Abundant Life Evangelistic Media Ministry (ALEMM) – Using 21st century technology to reach our neighbors and the globe.

- Abundant Life Ministries of National Destiny (ALMOND) – Ministerial Fellowship Organization & Missions Department of Abundant Life Christian Center.

The Spirit of a builder (Ezra 1:5) rests upon Pastor Walter Hallam. From the church's very inception, Abundant Life Christian Center has been known around the world for its hospitality, ministry of helps, and its spirit of excellence.

THE MISSION

The House of God - Abundant Life Christian Center has been in a perpetual state of building and remodeling to accommodate a continually growing congregation. The powerful anointing present at Abundant Life Christian Center has drawn men and women from all across Galveston County, Houston, and the Texas upper Gulf Coast, creating a large and dynamic body of believers. Never before has Galveston County seen such a revival and growth in a single New Testament church. The move of God at Abundant Life Christian Center is in part due to the pastor's desire to minister to the entire region, crossing all social and economic barriers in order to proclaim the gospel.

Pastors Walter and Cindy Hallam and the Abundant Life family's love for all people, regardless of ethnic background, is evidenced by the fact that the congregation is made up of a greatly diverse group of people representing every part of society. In addition to the warm welcome offered to all newcomers, the tangible presence of the Holy Spirit draws many from afar. Hundreds of healing miracles have been experienced as a result of men, women and children being touched by God while in services at Abundant Life. Over the years thousands of souls have been saved during the services at Abundant Life Christian Center. For example, in December of 1994 more than 3,000 people gave their lives to Jesus during a five-day crusade, and over 1,000 people gave their lives to Jesus during October of 2006.

Equally powerful is the evidence of God's provision for financial increase. The families of Abundant Life Christian Center have experienced phenomenal growth of personal and business income as they have given to build the house of God Abundant Life Christian Center has become synonymous with the place where "Miracles Happen!"

PRAYER OF SALVATION

God loves you—no matter who you are, no matter what your past. God loves you so much that He gave His one and only begotten Son for you. The Bible tells us that "...whoever believes in him shall not perish but have eternal life" (John 3:16 NIV). Jesus laid down His life and rose again so that we could spend eternity with Him in heaven and experience His absolute best on earth. If you would like to receive Jesus into your life, say the following prayer out loud and mean it from your heart.

Heavenly Father, I come to You admitting that I am a sinner. Right now, I choose to turn away from sin, and I ask You to cleanse me of all unrighteousness. I believe that Your Son, Jesus, died on the cross to take away my sins. I also believe that He rose again from the dead so that I might be forgiven of my sins and made righteous through faith in Him. I call upon the name of Jesus Christ to be the Savior and Lord of my life. Jesus, I choose to follow You and ask that You fill me with the power of the Holy Spirit. I declare that right now I am a child of God. I am free from sin and full of the righteousness of God. I am saved in Jesus' name. Amen.

If you prayed this prayer to receive Jesus Christ as your Savior for the first time, please contact us on the Web at **www.harrisonhouse.com** to receive a free book.

Or you may write to us at

Harrison House • P.O. Box 35035 • Tulsa, Oklahoma 74153

The Harrison House Vision

Proclaiming the truth and the power

Of the Gospel of Jesus Christ

With excellence;

Challenging Christians to

Live victoriously,

Grow spiritually,

Know God intimately.